CONTENTS

LIST OF ABBREVIATIONS

ADAS   Agricultural Development & Advisory Service
ADC   Aide-de-camp
CAP   Common Agricultural Policy
CPRE   Council for the Preservation of Rural England
ESA   Environmentally Sensitive Area
EU   European Union
FHDS   Farm & Horticultural Development Scheme
FMC   Fatstock Marketing Co–operative
GATT   General Agreement on Tariffs and Trade
IACS   Integrated Administration and Central Systems
ICI   Imperial Chemical Industries
NCC   Nature Conservancy Council
OSR   Oil-seed rape
POW   Prisoner-of-war
RSPB   Royal Society for the Protection of Birds
SAFE   Sustainable Agricultural Food & Environment
SAI   Scottish Agricultural Industries
SMMB   Scottish Milk Marketing Board
SSSI   Site of Special Scientific Interest
WAAF   Women's Auxiliary Air Force
WAR AG   War Agricultural (County Executive)

ACKNOWLEDGEMENTS

I am very grateful to His Grace the Duke of Buccleuch and Queensberry KT for his very kind and generous Foreword, and to Dr Joe Rhymer, an author of 25 books, who gave me invaluable advice, help and encouragement to start the book in the first place.

I am also especially grateful to my two ICI secretaries of The Leaths days. The first was Kathleen Bryson, a farmer's daughter who lived locally and was a fount of local information; she was a marvellous person to have on the farm and to have as my secretary. Kathleen was followed by another equally efficient secretary, Janet McEachern. Between them, a vast record of information was maintained, and it is from those scrapbooks that I have extracted much of my information. Janet originated from Islay; she married a banker and has moved around quite a bit, but fortunately for me she is again living in Castle Douglas and her husband is now my Bank Manager! My present secretary, Mrs Isabel Walker, has been with me for over 26 years. She deserves a medal because she is the only person who can still read my writing, which is in itself a miracle, and operates the ancient word processor. My thanks also to Yvonne Brown who came to my rescue at the last minute and has typed the whole book after a previous near disaster.

I do hope my readers will find the engravings interesting. The attention to detail makes them quite superb, and it is Ian Stephens RE I have to thank for his invaluable assistance.

I would also like to thank the *Galloway News* for allowing me to use two articles on The Leaths. These were written by locals, which was a great asset as their account of the day was very accurate, and they were also responsible for The Leaths photographs.

Last, but not least, my very sincere thanks to my dear wife Jean, who has always encouraged and supported me, especially over the last few months. She has been a tower of strength to me and has borne my vicissitudes with great equanimity and, I must say, saved the book from the waste paper basket on more than one occasion!

FOREWORD

by
His Grace the Duke of Buccleuch and
Queensberry KT

It would be hard to find a more engaging companion than Peter Maclaren for any excursion in the countryside. With his keen observation and widespread knowledge, fascinating anecdotes pour from him as from an irrepressible fountain. Even on a hilltop wrapped in cloud, seeking an elusive grouse, his sharp memory ensures a continuing flow of wit and wisdom.

It is rewarding to discover that this flow continues through his pen to paper, thus ensuring that they can be more widely shared and enjoyed.

There can be few individuals who have so excelled in successfully combining the theoretical and practical aspects of farming and good land management in many parts of the country over many years. To be a gifted raconteur is an added bonus, especially for his readers.

My own family has greatly benefited from his wise counsel and it is with a sense of real appreciation that I commend this volume.

1.

EARLY DAYS

Family roots, hoeing and humming

I was one of a family of four children born before the end of the First World War. My sister was the eldest, then a brother, then me and another brother.

My father was a true countryman and a renowned naturalist. I suppose one of his most astonishing feats was in the early 1900s when he made the first map of large areas of Alaska, with a team of husky dogs and a Chinese cook as his only companions. He broke his right arm very badly in a crevasse and set it himself so that he could carry on. The map stood in his form until the beginning of the Second World War. He also made a map of the Clyde Basin from a canoe, and it can still be seen at the Marine Research Station at Millport on Great Cumbrae today.

He was elected a Fellow of the Royal Geographical Society for his work in Alaska. He had gone there to find some organisms that live on the liver of a certain gull, and also to find other micro-organisms. For this he was elected a Fellow of the Linnaean Society in 1902.

His right arm was never really very strong after the accident and he was unable to join any of the Services during the First World War. He volunteered to be a spy because he spoke fluent German, but was again turned down, so instead he became Professor of Anatomy at Glasgow University for the duration of the war. He then stood down and became Professor of Embryology, and succeeded in being recognised as the world expert on the subject, terminating with a paper he read to an International World Conference in Holland in the early 1930s.

He was a remarkable man, achieving many other outstanding services to anatomy and embryology. For his work he invented a thermostat that he could rely on; but even more strange was the invention of the contra-propeller, which was widely used in aeroplanes in the Second World War.

It was interesting to find out that during that time top surgeons used to consult him before any major operation, a point that was later confirmed by the skin surgeon, Dr McIndoe, who became famous for his rehabilitation work at the East Grinstead Hospital during the last war.

This was underlined when my mother, who lived near East Grinstead, was asked by my brother to go to the hospital and see his Squadron Leader who had been shot down during the Dieppe raid and who had been badly burned. Poor dear, she hated hospitals, but she went along. To her amazement Dr McIndoe rushed over to her and said how delighted he was to see her as it was her husband who had not only taught him all he knew, but had also helped him in many ways. She was then given a conducted tour of the hospital by Dr McIndoe, which she said was a pretty gruelling experience.

My father, having proved his points on embryology, then carried on his work, but this time on cancer, which, sadly, eventually killed him; he was only 57. He was a brilliant but shy man, who was greatly missed by us all.

We lived near the Ayrshire coast looking across the Firth of Clyde to Arran and Ailsa Craig. They were happy days. We were surrounded by farmland and used to watch the Clydesdale horses going down to the shore after a storm or very high tide to collect box carts of seaweed to put on the land as fertiliser for the potato crops.

We learned to shoot and fish at an early age, and my mother often told us a story about my sister. When asked what her brothers did by a dear old lady at some ghastly tea party when we were very young, she said, 'Oh, one is a shooter, one is a fisher and the other a bugger.'

After a deathly silence, my mother said, 'What does the bugger do?'

'Oh,' she replied, 'he collects bugs and caterpillars.'

I was not that one!

My mother has hardly been mentioned, but she was a strong character herself - she had to be in order to hold her own. Her great love was gardening, and perhaps my own interest stems from her. She lived until she was 96.

I was neither a brilliant scholar nor athlete when I was at school. In fact, the headmaster told my father that I was a late developer, which I think meant that I was either lazy or stupid! However, with help from my father I got into the West of Scotland Agricultural College in Glasgow. Wye or Cirencester would have been more fun, but he knew I would not work if I went to either of them.

I had decided that, when I left school, I had to do something in the country. I knew very little about farming and would, first of all, have to gain some practical experience, then qualify in whatever I could and hope to get a management job. No way could I buy or lease a farm on £5 per month, which was my allowance.

In 1936 my learning days started in earnest. My first job was with a well-known potato-grower, where I learned about that business, and fortunately remembered the fertilisers that were used, as when I took the finals of the National Diploma in Agriculture in Leeds in April 1938, Professor Scott Watson was the examiner. He knew the man I had worked for and was particularly interested in his fertiliser usage. The classic textbook on agriculture by Scott Watson was the basis of our course, so I was lucky.

From there I moved to a farm in South West Scotland, near Castle Douglas, and remained there until October, when the boring work was to start. It was a mixed farm with a good pedigree flock of Border Leicesters, a beef breeding herd, mostly of Galloways, and a fattening enterprise for purchased steers and heifers. There were three men employed: a ploughman, a shepherd and a cattleman. All worked horses and produced the oats, roots, swedes and cabbages for the stock. The forage was conserved as hay made in the conventional way of cutting, turning, coiling (making into small heaps), then rucking into wee stacks (or pikes). The hay was swept into each ruck with a tumbling tam* pulled by a horse, then couped** all around and built with somebody on top. It was then tied with two ropes and left to weather. After it had dried it was carted on a ruck lifter to the stackyard and built into full-size stacks.

All the fat cattle and sheep were sold in the local market, which meant walking them the three miles; this was not always easy with wild Galloways or newly weaned lambs. I enjoyed myself, however, and was eager to learn. The farmer and his wife were very kind and took me to the Highland Show at Alloa. Unfortunately, as we arrived there I got a telegram saying that my father had died. I had to get a taxi and go home. It was a horrible experience, made worse because of his young age.

Prior to going to Glasgow to begin year two, I spent a few days shooting and playing golf before studying started in earnest. We were very lucky, as the local farmers allowed us to shoot over their land, mostly for rabbits and pigeons, but we also rented a small shoot. There were grouse, blackgame, a few hill partridges, the odd pheasant, snipe and woodcock. We never got big bags, but we worked hard for what we got. We got wise to the ways of the quarry and also learned that vermin, mainly foxes, crows, magpies, stoats and weasels, had to be dealt with.

We had good friends who were very kind to us young boys. They used to ask us to shoot driven grouse and do the odd pheasant days at Christmas - jolly good experience at our age.

---

* A tumbling tam looks like a large wooden sledge with five long teeth and a wooden back. It is pulled by a horse and driven up a windrow of hay until it is full, then taken to the pickle or pike and pushed up so that it is thrown over and the hay left at the pickle.
** Cast, thrown over, as a sheep on its back that is unable to get up without help.

I shot a merlin once - over 60 years ago I might add, long before the country was dictated to by uninformed conservationists. It swooped down and picked up a snipe that I had just shot, and was flying off with it in a matter of seconds. I wanted the snipe so I shot the thief with the second barrel. I have never shot another merlin, and would not wish to do so, as they are pretty birds and do no harm.

I was also invited to go north to do my first bit of stalking, and not only did I shoot my first stag but I also met a girl whom I rather liked. I went back after New Year to shoot hinds and to get to know the girl better.

The second year was not as much fun, for I had to study harder, and I came across all sorts of new things that I had never seen or heard of, so I had to settle down to work. I did not appear to be blessed with many brains, but at least I had a good memory. I took lots of notes and the lecturers were very good. I used to study six days a week, leaving home early and getting back late. I was damned if I was going to work seven days, so one day a week I had fun shooting or whatever.

Apart from not doing too well in two subjects, I got through the year. On the advice of the Principal I went to a farm in Fife, where I was paid peanuts of course, as you usually were in those days. I lived in the house, worked as a labourer and got my keep. It was a biggish farm and had a hill on it too. There were crops such as I had never seen or been involved with before. There was wheat, malting barley and oats, of course, for the horses, as well as seed potatoes, which I had to learn to rogue* and find out all about. We grew beet because we were very near to the Cupar factory. It was all very interesting.

I shiver now at the memory of having a hoe in my hands for seven weeks. There was one old man, over 70 years old I think, who hummed one particular and not very harmonious tune every day, all day - every moment I worked with him - so I got scunnered** with it. Every bloody thing on the farm was hoed, then we went back and hoed it again!

The staff consisted of the owner, a rather objectionable man, and his wife, who was not too bad. The two horsemen, who started at 6.00 am, fed the horses, then went back for breakfast. These men were not known as Tom, Dick or Harry, but as 'First Pair' and 'Second Pair'. One other man, myself and the 70-year-old turned out at 7.00 am ready to be given our orders. It was a pretty hard-grafting job - it was always a six-day week, and I was lucky to escape once a fortnight with a friend who took me out. He took me to church, then took me home and gave me a jolly good feed. We would then fish and have great fun. I stayed right through until harvest;

* When potatoes are grown for seed, all diseased plants are dug out as well as any different varieties that should not be in the field. The first rogueing is done by farm staff, but the second by DAFS (Dept of Agriculture) Inspectors who licence the crop as fit, or unfit if it not pure.
** sickened

it was the normal routine farm work - no glamour and no machinery such as they have now to help them along. Everything was done by hand, everything mixed on the floor and spread by hand.

In my last year at university various people came to lecture to us in the evenings, and if you checked them out you found out that they were generally going to be the examiners in the National Diploma in Agriculture. Now the National Diploma in Agriculture was much more important to the practical farmer than the Bachelor of Science, which was more for the scientific type of student. I was therefore very keen to pass. The oral exam was a bit of a problem because of my stutter, which was worse in those days, but I coped.

There was only one swine of a paper, Agricultural Engineering, set by S. J. Wright. He had been at Oxford University and was the person who had thought up the horrible word 'Dynamometer'. It was just about the time tractors were coming into use and not many people knew about them. I had driven one for about half an hour, I think, at Auchencruive. If you stayed on in Leeds for two or three days, after the end of term, you were told whether you had passed or not, otherwise you had to wait for the official confirmation some weeks later. I stayed on. Thank God I passed.

My mother came down to Leeds and we drove on to our new home - a very nice house she had leased in Sussex. It was very like our old home in that it was surrounded by countryside. Although we could not see the sea, it was still very nice, near to a small farm.

2.
SHROPSHIRE

John O'Nails

After replying to advertisements I was offered a job in Shropshire with a very well-known farmer who was a Governor of Harper Adams. He had three farms and employed young men like me on each of them - Assistants we were called, but we were really only mouthpieces, being given orders every morning and going on from there. It was a marvellous experience in a way, despite the fact that the farmer was not a particularly nice man to work for although he was a pillar of the local farming society.

All three farms were good lightish loam; sugar beet, potatoes, wheat, barley and oats and the one-year hay crop was the rotation. Lambs were reared on permanent grass, then beet tops and roots after that. The fat-stock was mostly Irish cattle, bought in the spring or autumn and fed inside on beet pulp then mangolds and so on. The interesting thing about these farms was the labour force. I think there were about 1,600 to 1,800 acres, and there were more than 60 men employed. On each of the two main farms there was a blacksmith, whose story I will tell shortly, and a foreman, plus an Assistant, of course, to see that everyone carried out his duties. The unusual thing was that all the work done on the farm was by piecework - long before anyone else had thought about it. Cutting hedges, or 'brushing hedges' as it was called, and mucking out the yards were done by piecework. Every mortal thing was done by piecework. The hours were long and hard.

The machinery we used consisted of two big International petrol-paraffin tractors. They were very high and you had to be more than 6 feet tall to be able to crank them. They were hellish to start and, if you missed it, it was quite a job to get them going. There was no machinery for them - we had to use old horse machinery pulled behind. All the grain was cut by binders pulled by tractors, but then we had a large staff - quite a change to when farms had to be mechanised in wartime.

The horses were all Suffolk Punches because the farmer liked them. I did not, and tended not to like horses anyway. They were fierce, wild creatures and we had some quite extraordinary experiences with them. One day when the hedges had been brushed and we were loading the wagons, the horse in the shafts suddenly decided to 'hop it', so off it went, down the road, flat out, with no one on it, of course. It crossed the main road and stuck the shafts right into the garden wall of the house where I lived. How it did not break its neck I shall never know - extremely wild creatures. I got a bollocking for allowing it to happen, even though I was nowhere near the horse!

I lived in the big house on the farm and was looked after by a housekeeper whose husband was one of the farm men. My pay was the princely sum of 30 bob a week, but my food was supplied. My orders were telephoned through early in the morning, around 6.20 am. We started at 6.30 and worked through to 6.30 in the evening. I had an arrangement with the local exchange to call me so that I was always awake when the boss rang!

There were two Bedford lorries, one on the main farm and one on the farm I was on. We carted the beet into Alscott to the beet factory, then brought wet beet pulp back and fed the cattle on it throughout the winter, along with mangolds and the hay we had made.

When I went there the first job was to cut the hay - one-year leys that were mostly ryegrass and clover - and it was a most frightful haytime due to poor weather. The whole lot turned rotten eventually. We carted it all in and shoved it in the bottom of the cattle yards and used it as bedding. The second cut was, fortunately, much better.

I used to smoke a pipe in those days, and one day when I was at least a mile from the nearest farm buildings and driving a tractor with a mower on it, the farmer drove into the field in a Baby Austin. Everyone had a Baby Austin at that time, and if we had one we were supposed to drive it on the farm. He was in a rage and flew at me. How dare I smoke when I was out in the fields, and did I not realise that I could turn the whole place into an inferno - 'blazing inferno' I think he said.

There was certainly one thing I did learn while I was there, and that was how not to look after staff. I learned also that if you wanted something done, you must first be able to do it yourself or, better still, show the staff how to do it - all very simple.

On Sundays the farmer would come round and we would pile into the car with him and look at the crops - sugar beet and potatoes and so on. I had always been used to 12 tons per acre being a good crop of ware in Scotland, and on one occasion, when asked what I though of a particular field of King Edwards, a field of jolly good potatoes, I said that I thought it would yield over 12 tons per acre.

'I never grow less than 16 tons per acre', he replied.

I do not think that was so, but the funny thing was that during that particular year a ban had been put on selling potatoes over a pound in weight, so you can imagine what he was like when we did not actually sell 16 tons.

Another day when he rang up he said that I must go into the sugar beet fields and pull out all the John O'Nails. As I had no idea what the 'John O'Nails' were, I had to wait until the first hand went down, and I saw the men pull out what I would have called 'fat-hen'. Then, of course, I joined in and we pulled them all out - in all the fields.

The farmer had a happy knack of coming round and making everything appear 'never quite right'. We seemed to be forever making a nonsense of something or other, or had pulled out all the sugar beet! I remember, too, at hoeing time, how we were expected to leave 33,000 plants per acre, even in those days. (Throughout the book I refer to acres - hectares had not been introduced, certainly not in the UK.) The nature of the man always came out, but you learned to live with it. All the crops were good - excellent, in fact.

We used the Bedford lorries on two of the farms to cart around all the sheep and cattle. One day he rang me up and said he had bought some lambs at Kidderminster, which was quite a long way from the farm, and would I go and fetch them? I put on the sides of the lorry and off I went to find the lambs. I loaded them on to the wagon and drove back, thinking I had done quite well. The following morning he rang me up and enquired as to how I had got on, and had I put the lambs in the right field? I said 'Yes' to all his questions. Then he said, 'By the way, you were driving much too fast'. I said I did not think so, but then he floored me by adding that he had been following me in the Baby Austin and that I must have been doing 60 miles per hour. Well, I am damn sure a Baby Austin could not do 60 miles per hour, and I am *bloody* sure the Bedford lorry could not do 60 miles per hour either. Little things like that used to niggle and become a bore.

Then it was harvest time. There were two International tractors with a horse-drawn binder with a man on the back. All went well for a bit, then one day, war having been declared by this time, the farmer said that the wheat sheaves we were making were too small.

I knew that the only way we could alter the size of the sheaves was to adjust a thing at the side of the binder, and as a last resort we could bend the tongue down and this would also produce a larger sheaf before the knotter tied it. After we made adjustments he said that they were still being made too small. I did not know what the hell I was going to do, so I fiddled again, but to no avail. Eventually I took the tongue off and went to see the blacksmith (mentioned earlier), and he bent it and put a bit of weight on it and we put it back on again. Now the sheaves produced were very big - more like straw batons. The farmer came into the field and was furious because they were far too big. I told him very politely what he could do with the sheaves - which he was obviously not prepared to do! We parted, therefore, not on the best of terms!

3.
WADHURST

Pigs at 4.00 am

Shortly before I left Shropshire I happened to hear that people with degrees were being called up and had to go to the Natural History Museum at Kensington in London to be interviewed by a panel of people that consisted of an Admiral as Chairman, high-ranking Army and Air Force Officers and a chap from the Labour Exchange. I duly went for an interview, but was told that I might have to wait for a while. Not being a very patient man, I asked the Chairman what was going to happen, and he said, 'I will tell you, young man. You will be called up in four years' time and you will be told to grow dandelions in No Man's Land.'

I do not think he realised then how prophetic his words were, for four years later, when farming at Ampleforth, I was indeed called up! I had failed my medical before the start of the war because of asthma, and when I was called up I went to see the doctor in York, whom I knew quite well by then because I used to shoot with him. I still had asthma, and as I was also in a reserved occupation, of course, I was marked down as C3 and was never called up again.

After Shropshire I found a new job on a farm in Wadhurst, Sussex. It was a small farm that was being re-built or renovated. It was a dairy farm, and new buildings were being put up. They were mostly up, in fact - for 80 cows, I think it was. It was to be a two-man affair, and I was to be Assistant. There were also 300 pigs of various breeds, plus a fattening unit, and I looked after this. The cows were milked three times a day and it was a seven-day-a-week job, but still the same handsome sum of 30 bob a week!

I stayed in a roadman's cottage just over a mile from the farm. Unfortunately it was at the top of a hill and the farm was at the bottom.

It was now the winter of 1940/1, which was very, very cold and very frosty. It was easy to cycle to work, but it was absolute hell cycling back up the hill. It made farming extremely difficult.

The owner of the farm had, I think, made his cash some other way, because he lived in a very nice old house at the bottom of the hill! I remember that he had a wonderful open fire, because we had to cut the logs. It had to be ash logs and they had to be exactly 3 feet long. There were two seats beside the fire, so you were assured of a very nice warm-up if you were ever asked into the house. One day during the frightfully hard, frosty weather, we were amazed to find all the pipes looking as if a bull had been let loose. The whole place had frozen up. It was really the most extraordinary sight to see all those pipes in the loose-boxes, and even in the byres, all twisted with the frost.

It was a 4.00 am start. My first job was to feed 300 pigs - bacon pigs - and to be faced at 4 in the morning by 300 pigs was really not my idea of heaven. I used to feed them, then went in and helped with the milking. We were finished by about 8.00 am. Everything was washed up and we were off. I cycled up the hill and had breakfast in half an hour, or what-ever it was, then cycled down again to muck out the pigs and sort out one or two things, help with the dairy chores, then go back home again.

There was always something to do there. Lunch was prompt at 12 noon and an hour later I was back down and to work again. Various other things were attended to, then at 3.00 pm it was milking again - the second milk-ing. By the time the milking was finished it was 5.00 pm at the very ear-liest. I then used to cycle back home, having said 'Goodnight' to the pigs! I would have my tea or supper or whatever it was, then at about 10.00 pm I had to go back down the hill yet again for the third milking! As I said before, going down was not too difficult, but going up was a trial, and it was very, very cold weather. I got to bed, if I was lucky, at about midnight. This went on for seven days a week and became - interesting, yes, every job on the farm was interesting - but rather monotonous.

Then out of the blue, in February 1941, the most extraordinary thing happened. I was not looking for another job, and was quite happy to stay there until I saw something advertised that interested me. Fortunately or unfortunately I got German measles. Now, where I got it I do not know, but I itched like hell all over and the doctor said that I was not to go back to the dairy until all the spots had disappeared, which was a week to ten days later. During this time I went home and there was a letter from the Headmaster at Ampleforth, where I had been at school, saying that they were taking on another farm and that he had followed my career - unbeknown to me, I must say - and thought that if I were available I would be the right person.

In answer to the letter I telephoned and said that I was very interested, but that I had German measles. So long as I kept away from the boys I imagined that it would be all right; they agreed and I had an interview.

They appeared to like what they heard and saw, and offered me the job. When I was fit I went back to the farm near Wadhurst and worked my notice, but in the interval paid a visit to the farm at Ampleforth to assess the situation and establish what was required to get started in May.

It was a place called Park House, Gilling East - a farm of about 300 acres. There was no electric light, no telephone, and certainly none of the 'mod cons' of that time. It faced north, and it was under a hill, so, as you can well imagine, there was very little sunshine around it. The tenants of the farm were to be there until the end of April.

To begin with I actually stayed in the monastery and was able to organise machinery requirements and sort out staffing from there. I ended up with two men, one of whom was a farmer who had given up rather early because he had not made a great success of it; he was to prove a great help to me because he knew all about farming in Yorkshire, which I did not. The other was a horseman - there were a pair of horses - and I was to be the tractor driver! There was already a tractor, and a tractor plough and other pieces of machinery were bought. In those days the only tractors were Fordsons on spud wheels - you were lucky if you ever got pneumatics. We eventually did.

I moved into the house and, fortunately for me, my mother had some spare furniture that she gave to me. She came up and saw me settled in, then I took on a housekeeper and from then on I was on my own. Thus began my time as a Farm Manager - a new dawn!

4.
WARTIME FARMING

Fighting the bull

The layout of Park House Farm was extraordinary in a way. There were 80 acres in three fields on the hilltop behind the farmhouse opposite Gilling Castle. The rest of it went down to the railway and beyond to the Holbeck. It was all very heavy clay and permanent pasture. From the beck it went through the playing fields up towards Ampleforth College itself. It was about 2½ or 3 miles across the valley, and I farmed this happily.

It was a broadening of my earlier experiences. We had two men and myself, and we grew barley, the first time I had grown it on my own. I bought a variety called Plumage Gartons 63 and when we came to thresh it the mill-owner said it was the best sample of malting barley that he had ever seen. His hands, which were always black, showed the grain to advantage. As it was the only cereal in the war that was not controlled at that stage, we sold it for £20 a quarter (4 cwt), which was a hell of a price. Everything was, I think, controlled at less than half of that, so we were very thrilled. But that was still a long way ahead.

At first we grew roots, mangolds and vegetables. We also grew wheat, oats and barley. It was a common Yorkshire rotation with the one-year ley under-sown with Italian ryegrass and red clover, which was fed to the store cattle in the winter. Everything had to be done manually. This was before fertiliser spreaders had become common usage; we forget these things. The fertiliser was put on to a horse and cart and you sat on the tailboard, which was put across the body of the cart, and a fellow drove the cart down the fields and the fertiliser was spread by hand. It had all been mixed previously on the floor. The only ingredients were muriate of potash in 2 cwt bags, which were usually as hard as hell, and sulphate of ammonia and superphosphates, which was even harder. You had to mix it, break it, then shovel it into the cart and off you went.

We also had a binder, an ordinary horse binder - you could not buy a power-driven binder at the time. We harvested by hand, including the stooking and so on. We grew hay, of course - also all done by hand. It was hard work. We bought in store cattle in the winter to feed on the hay we had made and roots we had grown.

Wartime created the greatest of problems. Everybody who was fit and able joined the Local Defence Corps - the Home Guard - which in our parish consisted of only 16 able-bodied people; they were the only ones left. We were not all able-bodied, but we thought we were.

A post on Gilling Heights had to be manned. It was a tin shed. So apart from working like hell all day, we were on Home Guard duty for two nights as well. Three of us went there from 9.00 at night to 6.00 in the morning. It had its funny side, though. To start with we had no uniform for the first parade - no tin hats, nothing. However, we had a marvellous major who lived locally, and he came to tell us what we must do. I was the only guy who had a rifle - it was a Manlicher 300, which I used for stalking.

He looked at it and said that it was a very good rifle, but could he see the ammunition? Well, the bullets were soft-nosed, so he said that was no use and was against the Geneva Convention. As I did not think that I would have to kill anyone in cold blood, I did not think that it mattered very much, but we had to play the game. I was amazed, being a countryman, to discover that when people lay down at the butts to fire at the targets some 100 yards away they could end up blowing up the earth about a foot and a half from the muzzle of the rifle. It just did not occur to me that such things could happen. I thought you put your rifle to your shoulder, aimed it at the bull's eye and hit it, but it did not apparently happen that way.

According to records the Home Guard was said to have suffered more casualties in the early part of the war than the Army because we were trained at throwing hand grenades that had long time fuses. Sergeants from one of the regiments would come and show us what we must do. On one occasion I happened to be in the trench, having thrown my grenade and counted one, two, three, when another chap threw his. It was supposed to go off after the usual length of time, and we listened for the thump when everybody would say 'Hurray', but the chap had dropped the bloody thing after he had pulled out the pin! I dived into the bottom of the trench, picked it up and flung it as far as I could. It went off rather sooner than we all expected! The other lethal weapon was a type of mortar known as a Blacker Bombard, which was always blowing up. That was my little extra to farming.

When we had a threshing day in those days, all the corn was built into stacks. The threshing mill and steam engine arrived the night before, with their own team of men. Lots of coal and lots of food were bought. There were bag carriers who would carry 2½ cwt of beans upstairs. I was amazed to see this - they hoisted them on to their shoulders and off they would go. There was a chaff person and the actual machine used was a self-feeder. Someone cut the bands and we threw the beans in.

The whole operation took about 13 people - it was quite a mammoth task. The threshing men arrived in the morning for breakfast at 6.00 am. This meant a real breakfast, which the housekeeper had to produce - bacon and eggs and the lot. The mill-owner then went out, blew the whistle and everybody started to work at 7.00 am. We threshed away until 9, when it was more bacon and egg for the mill men! The whistle was blown again and the threshing continued until 12 noon, when an enormous lunch, dinner or whatever they called it, was provided. That went on until 1, then back to work. Another break at 3, then a final tea before they went home rounded off their day. It was quite an effort feeding these people. Eventually that all stopped because we bought our own mill after taking on some more land.

I farmed there quite happily; it was hard work but rewarding and great fun. The land was very different - it was heavy land on the bottoms and light on top. The weeds on the top lands were frightful; we had to plough everything, harrow it and let the first lot of weeds grow, hoping that it was not too late. We then harrowed it again, if it was a decent spring, and hoped to kill all the runches - wild radishes - which were a beastly weed that we had in a big way on the land up there. We only discovered it when we ploughed everything up.

In February 1942, after a year there, I married Jean, the girl I told you about earlier whom I had met while stalking. She had joined the WAAF and by now had been all over the place, but had eventually been posted down to Coastal Command Headquarters. She was an Officer and had to go up and see her Commanding Officer. He said 'Fine' - he would get her moved to Marston Moor as a compassionate posting before we were married on 5 February.

The journey to Edinburgh was a somewhat eventful chapter. Jean and I had arranged to meet at York station and travel north together. To get to York you were faced with a long, stiff climb from Gilling village to the top of Yearsley Bank. The weather was snowy and my wee car simply could not cope. As necessity is the mother of invention, I had to have a quick think. One of the men took the Fordson tractor and attached a cattle feeder (one of the heavy four-poster type), put it upside down and used it as a snow plough to the top of Yearsley Bank, while I sat in the car being pulled by two horses. It worked, and I arrived in York before the prearranged time.

As neither Jean nor I were domiciled in Scotland, we had to be married by a Sheriff in court. He was a grumpy old devil who was disgruntled by the inconvenience of having to take a break from the case he was trying. After lecturing us on being too young, etc, he duly carried out his duties.

The next day we were properly married by the Archbishop of

Edinburgh and St Andrews. He was a friend of both families, and he must have made a good job of it as we are still together over 50 years later.

The weather prevented many of our friends from coming to the wedding. Conditions in the north, however, were not quite as bad as in the south, so Jean's father and mother, her aunt and her sister, who was to be her bridesmaid, made the journey without too much hassle. The wonderful old stalker who was born and reared at Culachy came too. He piped us in and out of the church, marvellously attired in full Highland regalia. He was a great friend and quite a character.

A few friends from Yorkshire braved the elements, and my brother, to be my best man, made his way relatively easily from his nearby base. He livened up the party considerably by bringing a bevy of WAAFs, one of whom he married some time later. Jean had only ten days leave. There was no glamorous honeymoon, but we returned to Park House a blissfully happy young couple.

Marston Moor was 20-odd miles away from where we lived, so Jean had to remain there until we started a family, which was as soon as we could. She then left the WAAF.

During 1942 the lay people who advised Ampleforth thought it would be a good thing if I took over the whole farming operation. The staff consisted of the man who drove and looked after the light horse and various carts; there were another two pairs of horses, looked after by two men, two general farm workers, a cattle man, a pig man and a shepherd. I replaced one pair of horses with a tractor immediately and, as at Park House, gradually introduced more modern machinery. The cattle man looked after the fat and all the fattening cattle in the buildings on the limestone land, helped by the general farm workers. The shepherd looked after about 300 sheep, half bred ewes, crossed with an Oxford tup, and the fattening lambs, which were wintered on swedes.

The sheep and fattening cattle provided all the manure for the following crops, which were wheat, barley, a one-year ley of ryegrass and clover, then potatoes or swedes. This was varied, but it was the common Yorkshire rotation of that time. This was before the time of complete fertilisers, and any deficiency was made up with straight nitrogen, phosphates and potash.

The shepherd also looked after a small herd of blue-grey suckler cows on some of the rough ground by the college. Through ignorance and probably lack of feeding we had hypomagnesaemia in the spring calvers. I had not heard of it before, but thanks to a good vet and better feeding we arrested it before too much damage had been done. The dairy unit had a staff of three and the garden, where most of the vegetables were grown, a further three.

On the other side of the valley there was what we thought of as a comparatively modern farm with 120 cows - all Irish Shorthorn, but they all had brucellosis. Attached to that was a piggery where we fattened pigs;

weaners were bought in and fattened on the farm with swill from the school.

Ampleforth School in those days had about 600 pupils plus all the staff and the monks and so on; there were over 800 in the whole place including the prep school at Gilling Castle. We had our own slaughter house, which was in fact the only private slaughter house that operated throughout the war. We were allowed to kill one beast per week and make up the required weight with a pig or sheep or two. It had to be worked out on the ration cards the week before, so if we had 813 ration cards that were worth a shilling, and part of that had to include Spam, we had to wholesale our meat and work out the fat weight of the beast and everything else from that. I had to pick the cattle that were to be killed, which were then slaughtered on the spot by a slaughterman who was brought in.

The carcases were not hung for very long - the meat was chopped up the following day and taken around to the various houses. We had a man who had a light horse and cart, which he trotted all round the place taking the meat, the bread and the milk to the matrons. The matrons always thought their share should have been more. There were at least eight houses, and there was always enough offal, etc, for them all, but generally I had quite a fight with some of the matrons. If they offered me a cup of coffee in the morning they expected to receive an extra kidney or something, but I had to be quite fair about it.

In 1943 I took on the whole place, which consisted of the land between the farm I was farming and Ampleforth itself, and three farms above Ampleforth on lighter land, where we grew the grain, potatoes and roots to feed the cows at the New Farm and the cattle we had there. Although there were no cattle yards at what we called the New Farm, there were three on the hill at the back. Again, because it was wartime and labour was scarce, we had to buy tractors and keep the farm equipped as best we could. We ploughed out most of the old grass - every acre we could spare.

Another annoying requirement was from 1944 until the end of the war, when we had to grow vegetables and were told by the War Agricultural Council from the North Riding that certain fields had to be ploughed up. One year, when we had everything planned and sown, we were advised that they wanted 30 acres of savoy cabbages planted as everybody was dying of scurvy, or so they said. We grew them, much to my annoyance, and they were damned good ones too, but in the end we sold only 11 tons - the rest were carted into the cows. There was simply no demand for them. Those were the sort of things sent to try our patience during wartime organisation. We grew a lot of cereals, all the potatoes that the school required, and all the vegetables we could grow.

The dairy was riddled with brucellosis, so all the milk had to be pasteurised. I therefore had to get rid of those cows and buy in Ayrshires; I came back up to Castle Douglas where I knew I could buy sound stock. We gradually got rid of the TB, but the milk still had to be pasteurised as there had been undulant fever (Malta fever) in the school, and extra precautions had to be taken. The Ayrshire cattle had to be tested for TB in those early days, hence the reason for buying mostly up in Scotland. Meanwhile we had to make sure that the dairy produced enough milk for the school and was made viable; I joined the Leeds University Costing Scheme to keep abreast of costings, etc.

In the early part of the war nobody talked about making silage; we fed hay, straw and roots, grain and beans. We grew a lot of beans then because it was the only form of protein we had. They were kept for a year and threshed in the spring. We had a hammer mill and bruiser and mixed our own feed; what cake we could get was bought in. This continued until we started to make silage on the original farm at Park House.

Shortly after that we decided that we should have a dairy there as well, so in years three and four we ran a dairy. We put in an Alfa-Laval bucket plant for 60 cows in the existing yards, and employed an extra man on the farm. Meanwhile we were asked by the WAR AG if we would take on yet another farm called Redcar, which was along a rough road near Park House. It varied from very light sand to a very heavy clay in the lower fields, but was a good farm so we transferred to it the cattle fattening from Park House. This gave me, in total, some 1,300 acres. It was 33 miles round in a car; I started early in the morning and by the time I had done my round and had seen what everybody was doing, or should have been doing, it was breakfast time.

This was the time of petrol as well as food rationing, so I bought a second-hand motorbike for 5 quid. This was a great saving as I had now become a silage officer. I went on a training course to Houghall Agricultural College in Durham, and visited farmers who were interested in making silage. The only silos that were easily bought or available were made of rings of pig netting; put up in sections, they were lined with sisal-craft paper. The grass was cut with a mower - this was before buck-rakes, but they did arrive shortly afterwards - and taken to the silo. Molasses were poured on every layer of grass until the final layer.

The only way I could demonstrate how to do it was at Park House Farm. The wire silo was put up and the grass cut. The treacle in those days came in 6 cwt barrels, and it took the combined strength of all of us to up-end them. They had to be up-ended in order to shove in the bung; before we up-ended one, we screwed in the tap half-way down the barrel, then opened the bung at the other end to let air in. The top was then turned on and out came the treacle. We had the barrel on a sort of trestle thing and poured the treacle into a watering can to show people how it was done.

On one famous occasion I was proudly wearing a pair of new jodhpurs and was showing the farmers what should be done. I opened the barrel of treacle and did everything right, or so I thought. I had screwed in the tap without any problems, had checked that the tap worked and then took off the tap bung. Well, I had forgotten that I had left the tap on and was leaning forward when the whole bloody lot came out and down between my trousers and myself. Thankfully it is not often that you get your private parts covered in thick black treacle. It was certainly not pleasant, but it was amusing. It wasn't easy to keep a straight face for the rest of the demonstration, but I managed.

Another amusing incident concerning treacle was when my wife, who is a very good cook, decided that the molasses would be jolly good stuff with which to make gingerbread. The head man of the Silage Officers for Yorkshire came to tea one day and had a bit of the gingerbread made from the lovely treacle.

'Gosh,' he said, 'this is marvellous stuff.'

To which my wife replied, 'Oh yes, it is made from the silage treacle.'

Well I must say he was quite a decent chap and did not comment or say that it was not supposed to be used for that!

The motorbike was a definite boon, but one afternoon when returning from a farm in the Pickering area, going as fast as the bike would go, two young soldiers in an army lorry, neither of whom had driven before, decided to turn right into a field. I could not stop and I went under the lorry sideways! The two chaps sat in the lorry, absolutely terrified; so was I, because I had seen the wheels moving towards my head. Thankfully it did stop in time and I managed to creep out. The bike was an absolute wreck, and I had a jolly swollen knee, which seemed to be all the damage.

A Baby Austin came to my rescue! Getting into it was difficult, but I was taken home and after the doctor had taken a look at my knee I was taken over to the school infirmary to have it X-rayed. It would appear I had water on my knee and would have to rest it a bit, but otherwise I was all right. It hurts me now, like hell, but it did not in those days.

Sometimes I feel that many people who lived through the war have forgotten or were never aware of the difficulties faced by farmers. I do not think that they understood that everything that was produced on farms, whether it be cattle, sheep, pigs, cereals or vegetables, was sold to the Ministry of Food at a fixed price. There was a sort of price review every year, and this gave us a very good idea of what each farm could or should be doing. In short, we were controlled by WAR AG.

In the early part of the war we were very short of labour, most of the young men having joined up or been called up. Those who were in reserved occupations, such as farming, had mostly gone. Most of the workforce consisted therefore of older people who were accustomed to the older ways, and this created problems when farmers were faced with the fact that they were required to produce as much food possible as imports had been so badly affected. In pre-war days farming was not so very important and we produced only a third of what we consumed, but in wartime the tables were turned and every available acre of grassland had to be ploughed up. More cereal production was demanded, so it was vital that we had a workforce to cope with it.

As a result the Women's Land Army was started in 1940. It did a remarkable job and we needed every one of the 'land girls'. They were particularly good with livestock, but not all of them could manage the very heavy manual work. Those who had farming connections were generally expert in the dairy, and they were all an excellent help with the vegetable growing for the school, and in general did a lot of jolly good work.

They came from all walks of life and contributed in a very many different ways. I actually had nine during the war, and although a book has been written about them, it does not really give the true picture. It contains a lot of poetic licence - that they were all man-mad, etc - but I certainly did not find that to have been the case, at least not with the ones I had. I do have to admit, however, that all of them ended up in the family way - but definitely nothing to do with me! It just happened that the farm was surrounded by Army Camps. I sternly told them all when they came to work that they could do as they pleased in their time off, but that there was to be no cuddling in the calf sheds. This, I thought, was a nice tidy way of saying 'Don't muck about, girls'.

I remember vividly one winter when the head dairyman was off sick for a few days and I had to give a hand to the two dairy girls who were finding it a bit of a struggle. One particular afternoon I was on my way to feed the Ayrshire bull we had, and told one of the girls on my way. I went into the yard and let the bull out for his food when all of a sudden he charged me and sent me flying. I was winded, but yelled as loud as I could and the girl came running. She took in the situation, promptly stood between me and the bull, ticked him off, and, to my utter amazement, he went quietly into his box. I rushed up to the infirmary for a check-up, but fortunately there was no serious injury. I am positive that had she not taken such swift action, I would have suffered a horrible mauling.

The labour force at the farm was supplemented during harvest time by prisoners-of-war - POWs. They were either Poles, who were good, or Italians, who were a bit of a loss because they did not like getting their hands dirty. Germans were also good, though they did not like the work much. They were usually picking potatoes in not very favourable weather. In the last year that I was there, 1946/7, we actually left a field of potatoes in the ground. First of all it was very wet, followed by a terrible winter of snow.

Over and above all the helpers, we had a school of girls who used to come and lift the 'earlies'. They were very good and, needless to say, were a great help. There was also a band of marvellous people, now known as 'travellers'. They did everything on farms and we relied on their help. They thinned and topped the sugar beet, and everything was done by piecework. These travelling people had wonderful names like Darky Harrogate and Soldier Ted.

There was also Thackery and Manners. I do not know where they lived, but they did have ration cards and clothing coupons like the rest of us. Thackery and Manners pushed a pram with all their worldly belongings in it. It was very ingenious because it was a pram with a false bottom full of ferrets. Obviously they supplemented their diets with what rabbits they could catch.

If a field of grain was dirty, they would say that they had 'looked' it. This always intrigued me. They had a hoe that fitted in between the drills of grain and they would go with these hoes through any of the cereals that were absolutely filthy. It was an expensive way of keeping your cereals clean, but it did work. In all we had an ageing workforce, supplemented by the Land Army, the POWs and the travelling people.

The Ministry of Food had a wonderful way of sending round the WAR AG people, some of whom had been potato merchants before the war. They looked at the crops and decided how much had to be kept for what they called 'end of season reserve'; this was to feed the troops abroad. At Park House we grew a field of Doon Star potatoes one year for this purpose. After harvesting, which was done with a horse and spinner in those days, we put the potatoes in a long pit - called a 'tattie pie'. This pit was built to about 6 feet high in a 'V' shape, had straw put on the sides and a straw bit on the top so that they could sweat. It was then literally earthed up with soil from the field and the potatoes left in this 'pie' until such time as they were required. They were then graiped* on to a riddle that took out the small ones. The seed, brock and ware** were left to go into bags. This riddle was worked by hand to begin with, so the handle had to be turned all day - damned hard work.

At the end of every season we had to keep a reserve, and in one particular year 200 tons of potatoes had been sold to the Ministry of Food. They always demanded immediate delivery but were actually supposed to give prior notice. Out of the blue, near the end of April, we were told that we were to dress the crop of potatoes, which then had to be hurriedly bagged and hand sown into hessian bags. They were then carted down to the railway station. We had to load all 200 tons of them on to a train for various destinations in Yorkshire where other potatoes were also picked up, and all had to arrive on or by 1 May to be distributed to the troops abroad. Each railway truck held only 6 tons.

On 28 May I received a letter signed by Dr Edith Summerskill, who was the new Minister of Food, it now being just after the war. In it she complained that 20 tons of the 200 tons sent had been bad. I knew jolly well that the potatoes sent were not bad, and accepted it as another 'try-on'. Had it happened some years later I would have demanded to have been

* A graip is a fork with flat rather than rounded tines for lifting potatoes
** Brock are damaged or misshapen potatoes, ware are clean and of the right size for human consumption.

allowed to inspect the potatoes. I would have taken a suite in the Hyde Park Hotel in London, or an equally fashionable one, and stayed there until I had seen them. In those days, however, you simply could not do that sort of thing, so I resorted to writing some very rude letters, pointing out that I could have wheeled the potatoes from York to London in the time it had taken them to report that 20 tons had been bad. After a lot of wrangling they gave way and paid up. It was a surprise to me and everyone else, but it was an exercise in how to fight your own corner.

The WAR AG chairman was usually some academic chap. In our case it was a man called Hendrie - Dr Hendrie from the West of Scotland Agricultural College - and I hoped that he might be an easy chap to deal with. I was on the WAR AG for the North Riding, being Silage Officer, and was often asked to do various other jobs as well. There was one famous occasion when I became very annoyed with them, when I was asked to take on Redcar Farm next door. Our agreement was on the condition that we got a Fordson tractor, a three-furrow Ransome plough and a power-driven 7-foot Massey Harris binder, in order that the harvest could be done without undue delay as by now our acreage had increased dramatically.

After all the farm sales were over in May, I was told by WAR AG that they could not supply me with the plough. I bought a three-furrow Lister Cockshoot on the black market, but still had no binder. According to WAR AG there were none in the country, and there was no hope of finding one; they proposed coming to cut the cereals we had grown with their binders. I thought this was a bit rich, because they had always been late with their own harvest and never seemed to have enough machinery. Nothing seemed to be happening, and I was furious about it, but after a while I forgot about it and went off to London to visit my mother.

My mother held a drinks party at which I got talking to an elderly man who seemed quite interested in my story of how fed up I was with the Ministry of Agriculture and their WAR AG. He said, 'Well, as a matter of fact I am the solicitor at the Ministry of Agriculture, and if you have a reasonable complaint, all you have to do is to come to the Ministry and ask to see the Minister, Mr Hudson.'

Next day I knocked on the door of the Minister's office, and was asked very politely what he could do for me, so I told him the saga - that the WAR AG were misbehaving and had failed to come up with the machinery that I required to run the farm that they had asked us to manage. He listened very attentively and said that he would look into it. Within ten days I had a telegram from him saying that a 7-foot Massey Harris binder would arrive at Gilling station within the next few days. I thought it was blooming marvellous! I had not expected that a direct approach would have had such an immediate result. I was not a very popular chap with the WAR AG after that. They felt that they had been slighted and over-ruled - as indeed they had!

Major Gordon Foster, who was one of the few understanding and good WAR AG officials, was also a wonderful horseman and judge of horses. He was asked to look at a farm not very far away from Malton that was farmed by an old lady. There was a lot of grass on the farm and he asked me to go with him to give a second opinion - a decision whether to plough or not to plough had to be made.

On the way there, when I was being given all the facts about the place, I enquired about the stocking, and much to my surprise I was told that there were only two animals, one a bullock of 40 years, and the other a 39-year-old cow. He did say that there was also a horse, which he would rather like me to see. When we arrived at the farm and had looked at the grass, the bullock and the cow, there in one of the fields was the most extraordinary horse. I knew nothing about horses, and I still do not, but Gordon Foster went into rhapsodies over it. It was the great Hyperion himself - he must have sired more Classic winners than any other horse living. I thought it was terribly funny. I had been called in as a witness who would say, of course, that the grass should not be ploughed up. That was a nice little touch of common sense prevailing.

While on the subject of horses, I must tell you about a horse I had just before I left Ampleforth. As petrol was in short supply, it was quite a bonus to be able to use a horse. One day, when haymaking was in progress in the field slap in front of the monastery, I took my horse across the valley. It had only one speed - flat out - and I was having great difficulty as it wanted to knock me off at all the goal posts on the way up, and to start with I could not manage to keep him straight. We went up past the cricket field, which had a cinder path running along the left-hand side, and on to the hayfield. The carthorse for the milk, meat, and bread grazed in this field, and was known to everybody, monks included, as 'Farting Jupiter'.

The haymaking went on all afternoon, and when we finished I mounted my horse once again. It was a lovely summer's day and a first-class cricket match was in progress at the time. As it was a school holiday lots of boys were around. The horse took off with me on board, down the cinder path, causing dust to fly everywhere, disrupting the match and upsetting lots of people. Thankfully one of the lads standing around had the good sense to open the gate at the end of the path. Heaven knows what might have happened if he had not. We flew on down through all the rugger fields, down to the beck. Again we were lucky because there were lads around and they opened two more very large gates. When my horse got its feet on the bridge, which was made of sleepers, it went even faster, so we shot off up to the railway where huge gates and fences awaited us. However, unbelievably luck was with us again, and the gates were opened for us by yet more boys. We fled across the railway line, truly flat out by now, and arrived safely at the house. That was some ride.

We worked hard, for they were demanding times, but there was also a lot of fun and a tremendous amount of interesting work. As I said, a lot of land was being ploughed. I ploughed all the land on one side of the valley myself. I liked the smell of soil. To keep up with the work I would quite often plough all night. The Fordsons with spud wheels that we used had little lights with three slits in them - lamps that you put on to the headlights. We had no cabs - we were tough and hardy in those days.

My brother, who was pretty fed up with sitting in his bomber being shot at by everybody in sight, was roped into ploughing as well. How much safer and pleasanter to be sitting on a tractor, ploughing. He came every now and again and thought it was great fun. One time, when flying in the area, he came and 'beat us up', and the girl we had as a maid was absolutely terrified and dived under the kitchen table. Worst of all the bloody sheep, in terror, jumped over the nets where they were fattening on the roots. My brother did not get good marks for that.

At that time ICI was interested in doing trials, so we used all their available seed dressings and did any trials that had to be done. We used their fertilisers, too, and we longed for the day when they would make something other than sulphate of ammonia. Shortly afterwards they did produce nitro-chalk, wonderful stuff, which was in smaller bags and the prills (or granules) made it easier to spread.

Towards the end of the war, about 1945, ICI also produced some wonderful stuff called Cornland Cleaner, which is now known as Agroxone. It was produced by two people at Jealott's Hill who later became friends of mine. I always thought that they should have received a knighthood or some such honour, because it was one of the most important things that ICI ever developed. When it came out at first it was in the form of a powder, which made it very difficult to spread because we had only plate-type fertiliser spreaders. The fertiliser went from the box down to the plates and it sort of trickled out, the plates going round only very slowly.

ICI knew all about my silage-making reputation, so I was invited over to Billingham, near Stockton-on-Tees, to meet Dr Alexander Fleck, who was the chairman of the Agricultural Division. He was a Scot, born in Ayrshire I believe, and was at that time one of the greatest brains in the United Kingdom.

Jean drove me to Stockton and I went to Norton Hall where I was to meet Dr Fleck; his Public Relations Officer was there as well. I spent several hours with them, and not the half hour or so I had expected. Meantime Jean was wondering what the hell had happened to me. Dr Fleck did indicate that ICI was very keen to expand on the agricultural side; he was on the main board, being a Vice-Chairman of the company. In his opinion more fertiliser should be produced to grow more grass, which he thought was the most important crop of all.

ICI was certainly becoming stronger in the fertiliser trade at that time, and had made the first of the complete fertilisers. The company wanted to buy three farms in the West: one Somerset way and possibly one in the Cheshire area, as they had farms there already. They proposed appointing three farm managers, so I confirmed that I would be interested. Sure enough, the advertisement appeared in February 1945, I duly applied and was granted an interview.

I went to London and one of the men on the interview board, who was later to become a great friend to this day, was Dr Robert A. Hamilton. He was a very well-known and very erudite man, and he became our great supporter. A short time later I received a letter saying that a great number of people had been interviewed and that competition was high, but as they had not yet bought the farms there was nothing to offer. I was annoyed and I wrote the sort of letter that you write at night and tear it up in the morning, asking why the hell they had trailed me down there when I should have been sowing spring wheat. As far as Jean and I were concerned, we thought that was the end of the matter. Not a bit of it - ICI rang up the Headmaster at Ampleforth College in December, saying that they wanted to speak to me.

I was asked a few questions on the telephone, including how far it was from York, as I would be expected to meet the chap who was coming to see me, who was the Senior Farms Manager. When I said half an hour, I think he must have been impressed, as it was 18 miles away, and I am sure he did not think that anyone driving an old clapped-out car such as mine could do it in that time. I did it.

I showed him around the main farms, the two dairies and the rest of the farms. He was obviously quite impressed, and even more so when I stopped to put petrol in the car on the way to the pub, and simply said, 'Fill it up, Frank'. I must have had an arrangement or coupons lying there. Anyway, he obviously reported back to Bob Hamilton that I was a suitable chap, for just after that I was offered the job.

When asked what salary I might expect, I reckoned that since I had got married on £300 a year and was now earning £500 a year, £1,000 a year, plus the usual perks, might be in order! To my amazement, they agreed to this.

When we had agreed to go to Ampleforth, the appealing thing to us had been the promise of a move across the valley to the ex-manager's house at a later date. This house had electricity, telephone and all 'mod cons', which Park House did not. This would have been bliss for Jean and our two boys, as Park House was pretty primitive. The opening of seven gates every time I used the car was also a great nuisance, and it was 6 miles to the Home Farm at Ampleforth.

To date this promise had not been upheld, and did not look likely to be. The seeds of discontent had therefore been sown, so I readily accepted the position of Farm Manager at Dairy House Farm in Cheshire. Just before the end of my time at Ampleforth, in February 1947, I went down to Dairy House to look at it and to see what was ahead of me. It had been a pretty rough, cold, wet winter. I went by train in the morning, changing at Manchester for Crewe, where I was met. I was then taken to Middlewich,

5 or 6 miles by road. I had a look at the farms and caught the train back quite early. It was due to arrive in York at about 9.00 pm.

At some point in the journey it had started to snow, so by the time Jean had come by car to the station for me, conditions had worsened and she had to wait, poor thing, until after midnight. We were stuck in a snow-storm. Everything had ground to a halt, including the heating. All we wanted to do was to get home, and to the children, but all routes appeared to be impassable.

We knew that Brandsby Bank would be completely snowed up, but we gave it a try. Eventually we had to give up and return to Brandsby and knock up some friends who lived in the Old Rectory, who very kindly put us up for the night. The following morning Jean was dying to get home to nanny and the two boys, so she started to walk over the fields and up Brandsby Bank, and had not been long on the way when she met a soldier who was anxious to get back to Helmsley. They walked on and met up with the man who went round with orders from Collinson's of York, a local shop. The three of them walked together across the fields.

Meanwhile I thought I should try to get the car out. By some miracle I managed to get down one of the side roads, Lord knows how because the snow had blown into all the roads. It was a surprised trio who found that I had arrived in Gilling before them.

The fields were reasonably clear, but the snow had blown right in over the top of the road. The Reliance bus that went from York to Helmsley was completely snowed up and you could hardly see it at all. The thresh-ing mill had got stuck in front or behind it and you could not see that either. All you could see was the top of the telegraph poles - it was a fair-ly frightening sight. When we did eventually arrive home it was a great relief to find that all was well there.

Dairy House had all modern conveniences, which was to be a great help to Jean, so we looked forward to the move with great enthusiasm.

5.
DAIRY HOUSE
Imperial, Chemical and a christening

When we got to Lea Head, our new home in Cheshire, on the Middlewich to Crewe road, we found it all quite flat and horrifically boring after being used to hilly countryside with rather special views. Anyway, you get used to all things if you stay long enough.

There were two farms: Lea Head, where there were no cows at all, and Dairy House, which was being built. The 'shippons', as they used to call the byres in those days, were completed, and they could accommodate, if I remember rightly, 120 cows, 60 on each side, which were machine-milked into buckets. The bull pens and the calf pens were still being made and the place was really just starting.

It had been farmed by the Alkali Division of ICI, which owned a lot of land in that area. The Alkali Division at Northwich was the original Brunner Mond place where they started many years before to make soda ash from the brine extracted from below the ground and the limestone brought from ICI quarries at Buxton in Derbyshire; they made other chemicals there as well. In those days it was the Alkali Division that looked after us and did all our ordering. They were also the architects for the new place, but it took me some time to get it in order - new fences, gates and so on.

One of my first tasks was to get those things started, but within a week of being there I looked at the dairy cows with great care and interest and discovered that they did not appear to be in calf, although they had calving dates in front of them on the blackboards. I asked the men about it and they said that they did not think they were, so I telephoned the vet, whom I did not take to very much, and whom I eventually sacked, replacing him with another who was a master at pregnancy diagnosis. His name was Jimmy McWilliam - a Scotsman of course - working at Nantwich. He confirmed not only that they were not in calf, but also that they had a rather horrible sort of VD called granular vaginitis. It meant that we could no longer use bulls on the cows, so we had to start our own artificial insemination (AI), which is not the easiest thing to learn in a day or two. We did, however, manage it.

To go back for a moment, I reported the situation to my boss, Dr Bob Hamilton, ringing him up in fear and trembling. However, being a very down-to-earth, practical man, he said, 'Right, I will be up on Monday. I want the ex-farm manager to be there.' (He had joined the Milk Board by then.) 'I want the vet there, and I want the architect from the Alkali Division there.'

Sure enough they all arrived at our house. I have never sat through such a grilling and such a bollocking. Bob sent the ex-manager, vet and architect all off with fleas in their ears - quite demoralising. I remember saying to him that if I ever made any mistakes, he was to tell me to resign immediately before I got such a bollocking. He tore those men into strips - wonderful to listen to when you were not at the receiving end. From then on Bob was a great friend to me through all the stresses and strains.

It took quite a long time to clean up the cows, but a year or two after the outbreak of granular vaginitis at Dairy House we were able to use a natural service. At about the same time we took over the tenancy of Lea Hall Farm, the adjacent ICI Alkali Division farm. The tenant moved out and we had to spend quite a lot getting it back into shape, enlarging the 'shippons' to hold more cows, altering the dairy and making various other improvements to the farm. We wanted to get them into shape ready for the original plan, which was to be applied not only to Henley Manor but also Dairy House and The Leaths at Castle Douglas in Scotland, which we had actually bought in 1948. We were being prepared for trial - No-Nitrogen Farm B and With-Nitrogen Farm A. It obviously took a long time to get potash and phosphate levels right and everything else in order, but we were then ready to get started.

The difference was that on Farm A we had a grass-drying plant and on Farm B we did not, so we made all the forage into hay, and the same principle applied down at Henley Manor, where we made it into silage. At The Leaths we made it into hay prior to silage being introduced. The spare land we had on both farms was used to grow a small acreage of cereals - wheat at Dairy House, oats another time and maize, which did not do very well as the crows ate it. On the other farm we grew cereals too, and the year we started we grew a field of potatoes. I cannot think why we grew potatoes, but we did. However, once the farms were going we ran each with a different staff except for haymaking, drying grass, etc. The dairy side was run on its own. The total size of the two farms was about 360 acres.

We had parties of farmers in those days coming to Dairy House from various regions of ICI. The Southern Region, based in London, sent up parties of 30 to 40 farmers, while the Midland Region, based in Shrewsbury, would also send parties, quite a lot from Wales. The Northern Office in Manchester brought farmers from there and from the North of Scotland.

In those days I did not have a full-time secretary, so we have no records of what went on so, coupled with the fact that ICI has gone through many changes since then, and valuable papers relevant to the farms have been destroyed. They were certainly not to be found at Alkali, Plant Protection, Billingham or Jealott's Hill, so I cannot say anything more about what happened during that time. The only thing that I can say is that it was a well-run farm.

We had more than one excitement. When The Leaths farm at Castle Douglas was acquired in 1948 the livestock for it was bought and a temporary manager was sent to look after it until the house being built for the Senior Farms Manager was ready. However, he left the company and I was eventually sent instead. I had only been at Dairy House for five years in all, but moving to Castle Douglas suited me well. There was good shooting on the farm, there was a very good duck flighting and a lot of geese, and it was back in the countryside in a brand new house with a wonderful view. However, before we did go there, we had, as far as I am aware, the first of the big International Grassland Conferences. It was presided over by Professor Scott Watson, Scientific Advisor to the Ministry, was organised by the Northern Office at Manchester and took place on 19 May 1952. We had people from all over the world - Europe, New Zealand and attachés from the various embassies. It was summed up as follows by *Farmer's Weekly*: 'The Grassland Conference organised by ICI at their Dairy House Farm, Middlewich, Cheshire, on Saturday brought together some 400 leading agriculturists in the country as well as representatives from overseas to discuss the most effective methods of grass production and utilisation.'

Before the conference we had a dinner at Winnington, where 57 invited guests were accommodated. The address was made by Mr Inman, Chairman of the Alkali Division, who proposed the toast to the King. The toast to the guests was proposed by Dr Fleck and the reply was by Professor Scott Watson and also Mr Cole-Tinsley, Vice-President of the National Farmers Union. It was a tremendous feast - wonderful wines and a very jolly evening.

During the run-up to the great day I had been working hard in order to get the farm looking decent, when my boss, the Senior Farms Manager, arrived. He did not really take very much interest in what was going on, and it was not until Bob Hamilton arrived that he noticed that I was limping. Unfortunately, in my haste the day before, I had jumped off a trailer and a three-pronged fork had gone through my foot. I had not gone to the doctor so Bob Hamilton said, 'You are coming to dinner this evening and

I will see that someone comes to meet you there'. I never thought any-thing more about it, got into my dinner jacket and set off. When I arrived I was met by an enormous matron who said, 'Mr Maclaren?'

I said, 'Yes?'

'Come with me,' she said, so I went with her, whereupon she stuck a needle in my backside and another in my arm.

'Now,' she said, 'go and have your dinner and come back to me at 12 o'clock, but meantime do not drink anything at all.'

If I could only have smelled the corks of the wine bottles it would have been marvellous, but that, of course, was not allowed either. I reported back as requested and got another jab, and then set off for home with my boss who was to take me to Lea Head. Unfortunately he was one of those people who never looked at the petrol gauge, so we ran out of petrol.

It was absolutely pouring with rain and I, like the silly so-and-so I was, got out of the car and walked the remaining few miles to the farm, got some petrol and took it back to him. I was soaked to the skin by that time, while he sat cosy in the car. He then drove me home, but the next day, the conference day, I was not pleased with him at all.

The conference was quite a big affair - by invitation only and men only. One man who had his own plane wanted to fly up, so one of the representatives who had been in the RAF arranged a landing space on the farm with wind directions, etc, so that he could land safely. But he arrived with a female - and not his wife. I think it was his secretary! I told her that it was 'men only' and she would probably find it boring, but if she went to Lea Head my wife would look after her. She thanked me very much, said they would be leaving again at about 3.00 pm and off she went. I did not see her again, but the man did leave around 3.00 pm. By then, of course, the morning session and lunch were over and acclaimed to have been a great success.

We split up into groups of 30 to 40 to go round the farm. We had put up special notice boards showing cows and milk churns on all the gates, providing information on numbers of cows grazing per acre and the amount of milk produced. Tea was provided around 4.30 pm, then from 5.00 pm there was a discussion time. After that everyone went home. During all this, however, the man's aeroplane was flying around - puzzling! It was not until I went home that I discovered that Jean had been asked by the lady if she would like to fly around the farm. She readily accepted and took the two boys and little girl up with her and was enjoying her 'fly-around' when she suddenly thought, 'My God, if we crash, the whole fam-ily will be killed!' I knew nothing about it.

That night Bob Hamilton said we must dine in Manchester, so Jean and I put on our finery and went up to Manchester and sat through a long evening. We got home quite sober, only to discover that my secretary had spent the whole evening carting the men about because they had discov-ered that there was free beer left in one of the marquees. The

Commissionaire had got completely plastered and was banished, so the men had a free hand and were absolutely 'fleeing', so the secretary, a rather nice girl, had come to their rescue. Another funny incident was that the foreman, who had been on the farm for years, had lost his false teeth and had a hell of a time finding them, if he ever did. Anyway, it was a rather good end to what had been a sweat, getting the farm ready for the big day.

Six hundred turkeys were fattened at Lea Head for Christmas-time, and 1,000 deep litter hens, both new enterprises. Some turkeys were taken to the local butcher and some were sold to friends and their friends, but it was a problem getting rid of the bulk of them. They were all rough plucked, but really beautifully plucked. I sold them to a firm at Smithfield and had to transport them. Our Bedford van was the type with glass windows in the sides - I packed it with naked turkeys and drove all the way down to Smithfield. I left early in the morning and called for the Senior Manager at his farm at Moreton Morrell in Warwickshire; we had breakfast then off we went.

The only thing I took with me for protection against all the black-marketeers and vandals was a .32 revolver for which I had no licence and which I used for trying to shoot white hares in the winter. It held six shots, I remember, and I put it on the front seat. We hurtled down the streets of London looking for Smithfield, and I had the revolver ready to fire at any silly so-and-so who dared to stop us. It was exciting but rather a long day by the time I got home.

By now Jean was having another baby and was attending the same gynaecologist in York as she had done with the other babies. The baby duly arrived and after ten days she and our new son, Shaun, were coming home, but first Shaun was to be christened at York, and one of the monks from Ampleforth was coming to perform the service.

Meantime, the Godmother and Godfather were travelling with me in the company Ford shooting-brake; we were to arrive at 11.00 am. It was a very misty and foggy morning, which slowed us down and made us feel very anxious. Fortunately it cleared on the Tadcaster road, so I put my foot down. We were soon into the outskirts of York, in the 30-miles-per-hour speed limit and going much too fast, when I was stopped by a burly red-headed Irish Sergeant. He asked to see my licence and asked why I was driving at such a speed. I explained that my wife was coming out of hospital with our new son who was to be christened and that we were running late due to the weather. He looked at me very steadily and said, 'It would be better to drive slower because it is not a good thing to arrive early in the hospital, early in the cemetery or early in prison. Please do not do it again because the "Super" lives along the road, and he simply hates to see people flying up and down the road. I'll let you off this time.' I thought it was jolly decent of him.

We were late, or course, but the christening went well, then we were on our way home. While crossing the moors just before going down into Manchester I saw a grouse on the side of the road. I stopped the car and asked for Shaun to be handed over to me. I took him outside, faced him in the direction of the grouse and told him that there was the finest game bird that ever flew, and that he must remember that.

Six weeks later, we headed for The Leaths. It is always rather sad when it comes to leaving a place, for by then you have formed a rapport with your men and have enjoyed working with them. Also, the uncertainty of the next step makes you feel somewhat nervous, but once the decision has been made, there is no turning back.

6.
THE LEATHS

The 'Baron' of Beef

We arrived at The Leaths, at Castle Douglas, Kirkcudbrightshire, on 7 April 1952. It was a nice house, but small for us because with the arrival of Shaun we had a family of four - jolly hard on my poor wife.

It was a good farm - 506 acres including woods, roads, etc. The woods were eventually planted again for they had been felled during the war. The soil type was light to medium with underlying rocks appearing on the surface. In this part of the world, known as Knowes, the soil was shallow and prone to drought if we did happen to have a dry year. The rainfall was about 40 inches, which was the average for the years that we were there, and the farm was only about 150 feet above sea level.

It was a difficult farm to handle in lots of ways because many of the fields were extremely hilly. When combines and silage-making equipment were introduced it was quite dangerous, and work could become very slow. I remember the Principal of the Royal College, Cirencester, coming to the farm and giving me a long talk, saying that farmers did not really understand that they had to do everything in the most economical way they could and that they must study time and work motion carefully.

He then went on to say that when you cut a field of cereals you must cut it diagonally. I quizzed him on this, and he said, 'That is the most economical way, and that is the way you will get the highest yield from the crop.' The first thing that I did was to take him down to a field of over 20 acres that was very steep on the north and south sides. East to west started fairly flat but by the time you got to the west end it was extremely steep and it had very little runway to escape when you came down the hill. When the Principal saw this field he became rather less adamant about diagonal harvesting.

The slope of the hill was in fact 1:4 - quite alarming when you felt your tractor or combine beginning to run away with you. We did eventually have the field in barley, having by then bought a Claas combine. It was a bagger, so I put my two sons on the back so that they could look after the bags, took the controls myself, and with fear and trepidation went down this 1:4 slope thinking that any minute we would run away and be 'couped'. However, we got down without incident and I knew then that it was perfectly safe to let other people do it. After that we learned how to cope and live with these hills, and when we introduced silage-making we were careful when using the machinery not to go into the fields that we could not safely handle.

The first few months that I was there we had to repair dykes and generally get the farm into some sort of shape, and by that time I had sorted out labour. It was not until the autumn that we decided what we must do. Before that there was a staff of ten. Three were dairy people employed in different ways - I called them 'professional' dairymen. They were paid a percentage of the milk cheque every week and they paid for their help. In this case there was one man with a daughter and another two men, making four of them in all.

I thought it was a damned useless system if we were going to do what we planned to do - to farm as two separate farms, farm A and farm B. I advertised in the autumn as the dairyman who was there had left, and we got a totally new staff. Most of them were there until the very end.

We farmed the A and B system from the autumn of 1952 until 1957. It proved to be a very difficult system from which to get decent records because half of the farm had no nitrogen at all and the other half did. There was a grass-drier; we used it on both sides. It was used in all kinds of weather, but whenever the sun shone and it looked like decent hay weather, we made hay, so in fact the B farm, although it did not get any nitrogen, probably produced better forage than farm A.

Farm B also grew roots until 1957, when the whole system changed. There is an article that I wrote for the SAI magazine that explains all that happened at that time. When the A and B system stopped, we reduced the cows to 120 and reduced the staff from ten to seven. There were two dairymen, a relief dairyman who also drove a tractor, a calf-rearer and a shepherd (we still had half-breds and mules). The farm was then farmed as one, and we had two new covered silos built in 1956/7.

The cows at The Leaths were in two separate byres, from which the stalls were removed. We loose-housed them for two years, 60 on each side. After that straw became very expensive. We certainly could not grow enough or buy enough, so we put in cubicles. The slurry from the two byres was scraped into two pits. One was quite small; it had all the effluent and the other one was a big slurry store, and a slurry pump was put into this one so that only one of them had to be emptied every third day.

The cows self-fed on the silage and we used various sorts of self-feed systems, eventually ending up with a 'tombstone barrier'. This was a wooden arrangement through which the cows could put their heads. The difficulty was that they really *were* tombstones - if there was an overhang of silage above, it fell on their necks and a dead cow would be found in the morning. We lost two one morning, so we had to be very careful. Apart from that, all went well and in 1957 we installed an eight-stall herringbone parlour in what had been the calf house.

The other development was that farm A, although roughly the same size as farm B, had more grass than we needed, so we ran a ewe flock of 280. It started with half-breds, but ended up with mules because half-breds became very expensive to buy. We also had just as many lambs. We divided a field into paddocks - eight, I think - and again some were high-nitrogen, some low-nitrogen, and some no-nitrogen. Where there was nitrogen, we put on six ewes and lambs per acre, whereas the no-nitrogen fields were at three ewes per acre. The lambs were weighed weekly and dosed for worms, but some became ill with coccidiosis. The cure was a poultry coccidiostat, and it worked.

At that time the Royal Show moved around from one county to another, and that particular year it was in Newcastle. I went up to the advisory service stand - now known as ADAS - and I asked them if they had heard of coccidiosis in sheep. They simply said that there was no such thing, and would not believe a word that I said. It did not matter very much, but it did show that there was a tremendous amount of ignorance in those days.

Another trial just after that was to direct barley straight into a sward of grass that had been sprayed off with Gramoxone. ICI was very keen that we should have a try. Nothing feared, nothing daunted, so we drilled 60 acres. It was quite a difficult job to get the grass green enough early enough in the spring to get it sprayed off.

Plant Protection had produced a prototype Ferguson drill that gave us all sorts of trouble. However, we did sow the barley, it did very well and it did work. The weed control thereafter was not very easy, especially if you had couch grass, but all worthwhile. Later, when parties of farmers were being shown round, I was asked on one occasion if I could let a Land Agent bring a young Laird around. I knew him and did not like him very much. He was always frightfully pleased with himself - he had been to Cirencester and thought he knew all about farming. I was not very impressed. When the Agent eventually arrived with him, he was wearing suede shows and carrying an umbrella! I showed him this particular field and he had a look round.

Not long afterwards I had flu or something and was in bed. My secretary rang and said that there were lots of things to sign so I decided to get into my clothes and go down to the office. Having made the effort I though I might as well look around the farm. What should I see but a car in the middle of a field with three people in it, one of whom was our friend the Laird! They had driven through the gates and right into the barley field, where the barley was just coming through. I was absolutely fuming to think that anyone could be so stupid - I could not have been more angry. I waited at the gate until they came back and gave him and his Agent the most frightful bollocking, calling them by every name I could think of - and I knew quite a few in those days. They went off with their tails between their legs.

As years went on we improved our silage machinery. At the start we did have a grass-dryer, but silage was a new thing. We had an old Bamford that had to be pulled behind a tractor and trailer; it was driven over the swath and picked up the grass, which came over the back of it and landed in the trailer. Someone was there to fork it into place, then as soon as the trailer was full it was unhitched and replaced by an empty one. It was very slow.

The other thing that arrived at that time was the buck-rake; it was a Rex Paterson invention, one of the greatest inventions of all. Any self-feed silage was made outside on Knowes and Rock Heads. We simply cut the field from the inside out and buck-raked the grass into a big heap in the middle, using Rock Heads as a standing for the heap of silage. We put a fence around it and the young stock used to feed there. Those were early days.

As soon as some other machine that would cut and chop the grass was available, we were on to it in a flash. The first machine was a thing called a 'silorator'. I cannot remember who made it, but it was frightfully noisy and you could hear it from literally miles away. It broke down frequently and nearly drove us all mad. That was followed a few years later by the Lundell, the first of which was brought from the USA by a farmer from Kent. It was a wonderful thing and we used one right through until Wilder produced a better machine. This was before the double chop and all the fancy things they have now on the market.

The grass-drying ceased as soon as we stopped the A and B business, so from 1958 on we were making a lot of silage. We filled two pits for the dairy cows, another for young stock and another for the beef stock, which was a new enterprise. We then made vacuum silage. A black plastic sheet was placed on the ground and the grass put on top of it; another sheet was then put over it, attached to the bottom sheet by plastic tubing and sealed when all the air was sucked out. It was a very tedious job, but it did make decent silage, though unfortunately not on the scale we required, and the machinery left a hell of a lot to be desired, so we eventually stopped doing that as well.

We had to build our own sides for our silage trailer - ordinary trailers were really too small. It was all quite an effort, but it was our main and only forage so it had to be made to the best of our ability. We started early but always in a dry spell. We had a direct line to the weather forecaster, for which we paid a fee. When a 48-hour dry spell was forecast, all stops were pulled out and we made as much as we could.

This was before the days of proper analysis of silage. All we knew in those days was the protein equivalents and the starch equivalent. The pH was obviously important, and so was the dry matter. If you cut the grass young you were almost certain to have good silage. Before 1960 the silos had sleeper sides that could be lifted out of the 'gizentas'.

'Gizentas' were metal boxes that I had made in order that RSJs (rolled steel joists) round gate posts, etc, could be removable. When not in use they all had covers so that no hole was visible. There was a most helpful firm of implement dealers at the end of the road, and the two brothers who owned it were equally as enthusiastic and willing to make all of them. We should have had them patented.

The 'gizentas' became very famous when a good friend of mine built a big sheep shed. He wanted to use 'gizentas' and had applied for a grant from the Department of Agriculture, showing so many hundreds of them at £1 10s each on the plans. Lo and behold they did pay him the grant. It did our ego a lot of good.

The original silo that had been used for the dairy cattle now became a self-feed silo for the beef cattle. It was the silage from there that fed the dairy cows for the next year or two before we made the new ones. One was over the original midden for both byres and the other was a new silo built outside where we had the slurry tower.

We stopped grass-drying the year we started to make silage - 1956/7 - and after that it was important to choose mid- and late-season rye grasses to improve the grassland. The right varieties were very important - good varieties did not get disease or die back in the winter and carried on producing the vast amount required for all our stock. To sum up the work at The Leaths to date I have included in the Appendices an article on the Beef Unit, which I hope you will find interesting.

Our first big Open Day was on 18 May 1961. Bob Hamilton was in the Chair; by then he was the Director of the Billingham Division, which had swallowed up the Agricultural Division of earlier days. He was also a Director of ICI Plant Protection, of which he eventually became Chairman. He delivered the main address, then Richie Turner, who was Senior Farms Manager, explained what we were going to do for the day. Addresses started at 10.30 am and it went on until lunchtime, after which there was a tour of the farm in SAI lorries. John Macfarlane, Technical Advisor, SAI, explained the tour arrangements. I think there were eight lorries, but there were 500 people, so they obviously had to make several trips. A break for tea at 3.30 pm was followed by discussion time, finishing at 5.30 pm.

It was all highly organised, which made for an extremely good day. The discussion was open by George Mackie from Kirriemuir, a very able farmer who had everything, even ducks, on his farm. He was a most amusing chap and opened the discussion in the right way. At this point I would like to mention that I was most impressed when his father, the great

Maitland Mackie, made the trip to The Leaths on a bus with a group of farmers when he was 79 years old. He was a man of such experience and knowledge that it was a great honour for me to welcome him.

From 1961 onwards smaller parties of farmers were continually being shown round the farm. Before the Beef Unit started they came from before April until harvest time, then after the Unit got going they came from about February until August. There would sometimes be two parties a day, and sometimes I would have lunch with them, sometimes tea as well, but always a discussion afterwards. You will note these dates with great interest - I was mad on shooting and used to shoot all over the country in the season. Apart from that I was asked to give talks all over the United Kingdom, so you can appreciate that I was a very busy man, but I enjoyed it. I met very interesting people and learned a lot in the process.

Early in my time at The Leaths we had five bulls of varying sorts - mostly Ayrshires - one or two of them bred at The Leaths. One day they all broke out of the field they were in and forced their way into another, where they ended up fighting each other. I took a stick with me and went in with a young man we had as a Recorder at that time ('Recorders' were young men employed by ICI/SAI, who came to be knocked into shape by me and learn the hard facts of farming for three months to a year or longer). I approached one of the bulls, smacked him on the face and told him to stop being naughty. The others ran away, but this one stood his ground, then charged me and stuck his horn in one of my legs, knocking me down. My stick had broken, so I was defenceless. I rolled over, rather like a hedgehog, but he put his foot right in the middle of my face. This did not improve my looks or my nose very much - there was blood squirting out everywhere. The Recorder managed to move the bull away and all was well. After a day or two I went to a specialist in Glasgow, who thought they were the best 'shiners' he had ever seen; he straightened up my nose and made it work again.

After that incident we had beef bulls, which were very quiet and docile. They were kept in a field at the roadside and lots of people stopped their cars to have a closer look at them, so I though to myself, 'I will give these people something worth looking at!' I sat down on the back of one of the biggest bulls and filled my pipe and sat there, puffing away. You can imagine the amusement on the faces of the onlookers. It was a bit of fun and a good laugh.

We carried on improving our systems and increasing our stock until once more we felt we were ready for another 'Big Day' with much to offer. Unfortunately 2 March 1965 began as a nightmare. It snowed more heavily than we had ever known in this part of the world, and the roads were very nearly impassable. The cattle courts and all round the farm were under about a foot of snow on the flat and much more in other parts. It was an alarming sight.

Fortunately there was a change-over of Recorders, and two new recruits had just arrived, so they had to set to work such as they had not experienced before - shovelling shit and snow in order to make the place even half presentable for the following day's event.

Next morning at 4.00 am I had to go to the slaughterhouse with Frank Gerrard to see the beasts that had been killed and hung some days before. When we had chosen the required number of carcases and brought them back to the farm we had breakfast. Immediately afterwards Frank set to on the carcases, hanging up a whole side and cutting the rest into various joints. It all looked, and was, professionally done. The building used for this purpose was the one where visiting farmers gathered on a wet day. It was quite an impressive sight and, coupled with Frank Gerrard's expertise and knowledge of beef, there was much to be learned. At the same time we were hoping like hell that a miracle would happen and that the snow would disappear and all would be well. Believe it or not the sun did come out, and by the time the people started to arrive at 10.30 am it was a beautiful morning. The snow had more or less disappeared and the day before seemed like a bad nightmare.

Coffee or whatever was available, then there was a tour of the meat, the cows, the beef bulls, the beef cattle in the yard and the suckled cattle in a separate yard of their own, then at 12.30 pm lunch was served in the Town Hall. Some 400 people were fed on The Leaths's beef cooked 'en crout' for us by the local baker. It was rolled sirloin, all from heifers, and was jolly good. I cannot remember what else there was, but it was so bloody cold that I do remember putting a bottle of whisky on every table. Everyone seemed to think this was a good idea. I certainly did.

After lunch we adjourned to the local cinema for the Conference. It was an ideal venue. We had to move about 20 rows of seats in order to put a platform in place for the speakers, Bob Hamilton, Professor Mac Cooper and myself. Mac Cooper spoke about what was happening at Cockle Park, the Northumberland University farm, at The Leaths and in the meat industry in general. After that a discussion followed and much was derived from it all. The only trouble I had was that having had so many early mornings and having talked so much, I had practically lost my voice. When Bob Hamilton invited me to have dinner with him the night before, he told me to go and see a doctor. I did and was given an injection to keep me going for the day; however, I was warned that I could lose my voice for a fortnight. This, I have no doubt, was an absolute joy to other people, but a curse to me because it was the only time I had been invited to London to do a television programme, so all the might-have-been fame and fortune disappeared. Instead I had to stay at home and squawk and squeak, not able to speak for the predicted two weeks.

A booklet called 'Beef on The Leaths' was produced, despite very nearly not getting through to the printer because of snow. The one thing that was cheering and consoling, while I was laid up voiceless, was the tremendous 'fan mail' received, and the write-ups in all the papers, national and farming - the *Financial Times*, *The Field*, *Country Life* and all the others I could find reported on 'The Day'. A truly great accolade.

A book of all the press cuttings was started by my excellent secretary. I enjoy having a look at it nowadays to remind me of what we did and of the impact it had on beef production thereafter.

The Beef Unit was built up to 300 cattle and the dairy herd up to 230, so the whole thing was starting to expand. We had no room for sheep. The most important thing of all was the grassland. The grassland mixtures had begun to change in the late 1950s and '60s and had to be given careful thought. We went entirely into rye grass and used two strains - a blend of Diploid and Tetraploid, both mid-term strains. The early-flowering variety was not at all suitable. The two strains chosen produced a lot of bulk, and also provided a lot of good grazing, which we needed very badly. The system worked very well indeed. The dairy herd was increased not by breeding our own, which we found not very economical, but by buying in-calf heifers from a well-known stock in Wigtownshire.

At that time silage-making was also becoming much easier. We had flail mowers to cut the grass and a Wilder to pick it up. We went at it hammer and tongs and kept a gang going over the lunch hour - usually myself and a dairyman. There were no breaks and we did as much as we could when the weather was good.

As a sort of bonus I was asked by Bob Hamilton if I would have a look at the big suckler cow herds up in the North. I gathered a band of very good stockmen, renowned for their stockmanship and business acumen, and off we set. We started off at Ben Challum, which belonged to the late Duncan Stewart of Millhills, Crieff, who pioneered heather-reclamation and out-wintering. It was looked after by Ben Coutts who was an expert in his field and another great character. We had a great day there, then we headed for Inverness and on to Lord Lovat's vast empire. He had something like 800 or 1,000 cows, and the estate literally ran from the East Coast to the West Coast, which if you look at the map you will see is a hell of a long way. We went to a place called Braulen, up above Beauly, near Inverness, and had another marvellous day there seeing the cattle, how they chased them and herded them. Lord Lovat was a splendid man, and it was a day to remember, dining in the castle and so on. From there we went and stayed at Fort William.

Next day we went to the Great Glen Cattle Ranch. The man who owned the whisky distillery there had built up the place - again a very big herd of cows - and he had also reclaimed the heather. It was very different from the first place but equally as interesting; even more so was the rather good liqueur whisky we had at lunch.

Fort Augustus and Culachy, an estate inherited by Jean from her aunt, was our next stop. Sadly, however, we did not have enough money to educate our children and run the estate, so we were advised not to try. These trips were an education for us all, and the social side of them was a very pleasant bonus. Speaking personally, it stood me in good stead when I eventually started up my own consultancy business.

I was also asked by Head Office to escort around the country a man called Terence O'Dwyer from the Argentine, but who had been born in Northern Ireland. He was a wonderful man, and an ICI Vice-Chairman had invited him to come to The Leaths when on one of his visits to the Perth bull sales to buy Shorthorn and Angus bulls. At that time he was Chairman of the Australian Mercantile Insurance Company, had literally millions of cattle and many millions of sheep, and was delighted to take up the invitation.

I was picked up by a chauffeur-driven Bentley on the Sunday and driven to Edinburgh, where I stayed in a suite at the Caledonian Hotel ready to meet this chap off the early morning train. After he had freshened up, we took off to look over a farm belonging to a family whom he knew very well - the Cadzows by name. We had a most inspiring morning there, then we lunched with members of the SAI board. This took rather a long time, but by the end of it he was well informed on what they were doing in Scotland. Coldstream was where we spent the night. I was cashier - never had I had so much money on me.

The farms to be visited the next day were costed farms and the ICI Development Officers who looked after them were our guests. We went off to somewhere on the borders of Cumbria and Northumberland and did the same thing the next night. On the Wednesday we were invited to have lunch with the ICI Board at Billingham. Sir Alex Fleck was there, the Divisional Chairman and several others, and we had a great time. In the afternoon we went to look at a costed farm in the Yorkshire hills, and after that we drove down to the White Hart Hotel in Lincoln where we met all the people whose farms we were to visit the next day.

Early next morning we set off to see the first farm, which was on higher ground. We met the farmer and went into his office, which was full of gadgets and charts - it was obvious that he was very keen on flying. The walk round his farm was an interesting experience. At one point we went into a very big field of potatoes, which I remember very well because it was so very dry. He had a new fancy lifter or digger at work and I did not think it was lifting half of the crop, so I told him so. He immediately went back to the Land Rover, which had a CB radio, and ordered the foreman to come and check it! Our host was also a very keen shooting man, so he had planted a lot of hedges all over the place.

It was a beautiful day and when he asked if we would like to fly over the farm, we accepted readily. We were driven to a hanger in the Wolds; it was on a slope, so all he had to do was pull back the chocks and the plane reversed itself, so to speak. He started it up and we went to the end of the grass runway. He then radioed the RAF, and a very bored RAF voice said, 'Oh, you will have to wait, there are lots of jets flying around.' So we waited - Terence O'Dwyer and the owner in front and me in the back.

Eventually we took off, very sedately, and flew over the place. It was right next door to a partridge shoot, which I was very keen to see from the air. During our fly-around the farmer asked if my friend knew anything about flying. I told him that he did, and that in fact he had been a Group Captain in the RAF and had been based somewhere in the area during the war. He promptly offered Terence the controls, which he took over without hesitation. That was the biggest mistake of my life. I could almost have picked beans hanging out of the cockpit!

After due thanks and goodbyes we took our leave. In the car, however, we nearly burst our sides laughing at just how funny it had been.

We next travelled down to the Fens at Boston to a very able farmer who had two farms, about 1,000 acres of first-class land, and did everything right. The spinach that he used to sow after his vining peas cornered the market. Onions were also grown, and although he had started with only 90 acres, he had now increased it considerably. He had gone across to New York State to discover all about onions, and had bought the machinery there, bringing it back to help him grow marvellous onions.

He had the first wheat store that I had ever seen, holding over 1,000 tons. He had an old man with one leg who made all the cartons that held the cauliflowers, which were sold six heads in a carton. Potatoes were what they had previously relied on, but he thought it was only wise to sow other things as a safety net. He reckoned that 'tates', as they were called in Lincolnshire, would become socially undesirable, so he was anxious to find a replacement crop so that he could provide full employment for his staff.

An acre of glasshouses was erected every year for five years. He grew tomatoes on the hydroponic system, not like anyone else before. He also grew bulbs - tulips, daffodils and hyacinths. All these were forced in the house and ready to be sold by Christmas, then in went the tomatoes.

We were there in September of that year, and they were planting these bulbs out. They had been fumigated and were in what I thought was a deep-freeze arrangement. They were put in big tattie-trays, planted in the ground and remained there until they had sprouted; they were then put in a glasshouse. It was a most fascinating place, and everything was just right. We retired to the Black Bull in Stamford where an awful lot of whisky was consumed before we drove on to our next engagement.

On the Friday we went round farms in the Thames Valley, staying at the Hind's Head at Bray, a well-known hostelry. Bob Hamilton and Vice-Chairman Donald Scott came and dined with us, which was relaxing and great fun. The next day we went round the ICI Research Station at Jealott's Hill. This everyone found most absorbing. The day ended by meeting up again with Bob Hamilton and Donald Scott, along with several others for dinner.

On the Saturday evening Donald Scott entertained us at his home, then next day I was taken by taxi to the airport and flew to Prestwick. I almost fell out of the plane with exhaustion. Thank goodness Jean was there to meet me.

Earlier I mentioned that Terence O'Dwyer had been invited by a Vice-Chairman of ICI. This was, in fact, Donald Scott, whom I had not met until he came to The Leaths when he visited a Highland Show held in Dumfries. Whether or not he was sent up to find out if I was a suitable person to act as Terence O'Dwyer's 'ADC' I never found out. A week or two prior to the show we had been asked if we would put up Donald Scott, but when the time came we had a house full of guests as well as a full caravan - all our friends descended at show time. On the day Donald Scott was due to arrive Bob Hamilton telephoned, telling me what an important man he was.

'Look after him,' he said. 'What are you having for dinner and what are you drinking?'

I did not know what we were going to have for dinner, but I did know that we would have some decent wine.

'Well,' he said, 'that is no good. He drinks only champagne and the very best claret.'

I promptly replied that I could not afford to buy champagne.

'That's OK, leave it with me,' was his reply, and I did. A few hours later a case of Krug champagne, 1947, arrived. It was opened and drunk at once; thanks to Donald all our guests had a really good evening.

The Leaths farmhouse was quite small, with only one bathroom upstairs. There was our own bedroom, two smaller rooms with bunk beds and a playroom-cum-bedroom, which we used when we had guests. The remaining bedroom was for the nanny, and it was particularly small. This was the one that we gave to Donald Scott - we had farmed the nanny out!

The next day he went to the Highland Show, and the after that day he wanted to play golf at Southerness, so we arranged to meet there. I had not played for a month or more, but he, I was told, was a keen and very good golfer, so I was a bit apprehensive. However, luck was with me - it rained, so I did not have to perform after all.

That evening we were invited to friends for dinner and our guests were included. Donald, however, was dining with ICI friends in Dumfries. We expected to be late back, but Donald did not envisage a late night on his part. We got back about midnight and, assuming that Donald had already returned, locked up and went to bed. Not very long after we had settled down there appeared to be a shower of hailstones. On looking out, there was poor Donald locked out and doing his best to arouse us with gravel. It was a very inauspicious meeting with the Maclarens, but obviously he did not hold it against us.

Again while at The Leaths I was asked to go to Iowa because I was supposed to know something about beef cattle. I would have enjoyed such a trip, but the company would not let me go - quite infuriating.

However, the previous year I had decided that it was time for a change, so I had given in my notice. By this time - 1968 - the staff at ICI had changed: Sir Alexander Fleck had now become Lord Fleck and had retired, and Bob Hamilton had become Chairman of the Plant Protection Division and could no longer support or protect me against the new generation of ICI personnel, so I was up against it!

Immediately after the war a party of ICI people had gone to learn grassland management from the Dutch, something at which the Dutch were experts. They knew how to handle it, they knew how to make it into silage and at the end produce a tremendous amount of milk. The Dutch Ministry of Agriculture was always most helpful and worked very closely with the fertiliser people, especially those with experimental farms.

Such visits continued, and before I left ICI I led a party - the final one I went on - and we had a tremendous time. They knew that I was leaving, so we were wined and dined. The Dutch can feast, I promise you. They took us to a restaurant called 'The Black Sheep' in Amsterdam - a most famous place - and the meals on the menu were a 'Ducal', 'Royal' or 'Emperor', so it was decided to go for the 'Emperor'. We sat down at 8.00 pm, having had a few jars, and did not get up from the tables until 4.00 am the following morning after a lot of speeches saying wonderful things!

By now I had made up my mind to start up my own consultancy business, so before I departed from ICI it was thought that a 'launching party' would be appropriate. Every year ICI held a lunch for agricultural journalists, usually about 270 of them, so it was decided that this would be an ideal occasion to invite me along. The beef was to be supplied from The Leaths, so after killing a few cattle a suitable baron of beef was found - Lincoln Red/Ayrshire cross, beautifully hung, and just the right amount to feed such a number.

All the speeches held reference to the 'Baron' of beef and to 'The Baron' from The Leaths. It was a tremendous occasion, but there was only one thing wrong. All the press were there, but there was one empty seat, and that was mine. I had been doing a job in Fife the night before, heavy frost and thick fog descended and I did not make it! I was to have flown from Edinburgh and to have been picked up at Heathrow Airport and taken to the lunch. I was deeply disappointed. Inevitably it was reported in the newspapers with a note from Alex Yeaman to explain my absence!

Agriculture

'BARON' OF BEEF AND MILK FROM GRASS

by Alex F. Yeaman

Given traditional and well-deserved honours the other day at one of London's fashionable restaurants was a magnificent baron of beef. It came from a Lincoln Red-Ayrshire cross steer, 1,134 lbs at 20 months put on at a rate of 1.62 lb a day, a killing out at 65%.

The animal was bred and reared at Leaths, Castle Douglas, by Imperial Chemical Industries Ltd.

They were hosts at the London lunch, and the man who did the breeding for ICI, along with 300 other dairy beeves a year of comparable percentage, was Mr Peter Maclaren, 22 years with ICI, 17 as manager at Leaths.

But Mr Maclaren's long association with ICI and Leaths comes officially to an end today. He decided on an early retirement at 50 years to branch out on his own, giving up the management of one famous 500-acre holding to exert a management influence over 50,000 acres in the capacity of private consultant. Maybe more than one of the dozen holdings from Ross-shire to the Borders already on his books will become quite as well-known as Leaths is today.

For few men are quite so skilled, or articulate, on the modern management of grass for impressive outputs of both milk and meat. When he first went to Leaths the farm carried 120 dairy cows. Today there are 230 milk cows and 800 head of stock all told.

Mr Maclaren, Glasgow born - his father, a former professor of zoology at Glasgow University, made the first map of Alaska - is thoroughly dedicated to the gospel of better grass. He believes that a great many farms could produce a great deal more than they do.

'What was OK in the 1950s is no longer any good at all,' is a favourite opening gambit on the favourite farm outputs topic with Mr Maclaren, a graduate of the West of Scotland Agricultural College.

During my 17 years at The Leaths I was extremely fortunate to have a loyal and dedicated staff. Without them we could not have achieved the results we did. Some of the original staff are still around and it is always good to meet them or their wives. All the staff took great pride in their work. The grass was cut in perfect straight lines, and the ploughing was always immaculate, as was the corn drilling. They were a dedicated group of men, who were a pleasure to work with.

I remember only too well when the time and motion people were sent up from Head Office to see and assess how we fared. They watched the milking, they timed the slurry scrapers, then they walked behind the tractors at silage time with a true-metre-measuring wheel. This was to ascertain the number of loads and the time it took to fill and empty. The men were highly amused, and one said to me, 'They must be a lot of silly buggers if they think we are not capable of finding out for ourselves the shortest and most efficient methods.' Those were my sentiments too.

My secretaries over the years, one after the other, were also all good. They kept the books and the records straight, and ably shielded me when anyone rang up from Jealott's Hill or Billingham, saying that I was away for the day shooting! They always knew where I was, but as far as 'others' were concerned I was 'out on the farm'. I always spoke to the men before going off, and left notes, rude or otherwise, on my office desk after having read my mail. It worked marvellously.

As mentioned earlier, in 1952 all ICI demonstration farms were allocated a 'Recorder', a young trainee to carry out the on-going experiments. Their responsibilities included measuring the dry matter produced from various fields by using cages and cutting the plots with an autoscythe, looking after the weather station, which included soil temperatures at ground level and 4, 8 and 12 inches deep, as well as all the beef and milk graphs. These lads were a great help to me, especially if they were allowed to stay long enough.

The first, Jimmy Wardrop, was the best. He was allowed to stay until he went farming on his own, and this he has done very successfully. Some, however, were pretty useless, and had to be taught everything. I had to write a report on them for whichever region they had been allocated to, and I hated that. Most were good natured and we had some fun with them.

One tall and very spruce young man amused the men as he used to walk about with a rolled umbrella. One day, however, his umbrella was no protection. A party of farmers had just arrived and as there was a shortage of farm guide books, I asked the trainee to run back to the office for more. The shortest route was through the slatted calf house, so he jumped in, forgetting that the slats had been removed! He sank up to his moustache in evil-smelling muck. It was horrible for him, but it did provide us with a lot of merriment. There were other amusing incidents provided by our young Recorders, but that was certainly the most memorable.

7.
WRITING TALKS AND ARTICLES

Hot air and headlines

After the big beef day we had at The Leaths, I became, unfortunately for me perhaps, rather well known. People started writing to me from all over the place, and I was invited to talk here, there and everywhere. It became either very exciting or very boring. If you were addressing people who knew roughly what you were on about, then it could be very exciting. The most exciting of all was, perhaps, the International Beef Symposium, which Professor Cooper had organised at Newcastle University. It was a three-day event that gathered together experts from all over the world.

All the invited guests, some 60 or so, stayed in Newcastle and slept in a long dormitory-type place, so the chat went on well into the early hours of the morning. The evening before the official start there was a dinner at which Professor Frank Raymond, Chief Advisor to the Ministry of Agriculture, addressed the gathering; he was a very solid chap. I had met them all at Hurley, the Grassland Centre. There were some very good people there, amongst whom were Frank Raymond and Colin Spedding, who was the sheep expert. Both of them had visited The Leaths on a combined trip to the Hannah Dairy Institute and Dr Blaxter. The Grassland Centre at Hurley produced some tremendous work and was a great help to many. Colin Spedding is now advisor to the Ministry on a whole lot of subjects, including the organic side of farming.

The first day of the symposium was given over entirely to animal 'food digestion' - where it went, what happened to it, and how the animal used it. The lectures started with one by Dr Armstrong, the nutritional expert at Newcastle University. He gave us a very clear and lucid explanation of what an animal does with its food; it does not simply eat it at one end and dispose of it as muck at the other. I am afraid the ordinary farmer would not think about it, but it was all very easy to understand when it was explained in such a manner! Dr Prescott, the pig nutritionist, followed, and that completed the morning session.

The afternoon session followed the same pattern, but with different lecturers explaining to us, talking to us, and hoping that at the end of the day we would go away understanding it all. In my case, I regret to say, I did not.

Day two was taken up with farm visits. We went to three or four: the Moraley farms came first. Dan Moraley was a producer of really good stock out of blue-grey cows, mostly Irish and served by Charolais bulls that he had - in those days they were a fairly new breed in Britain, and we had a bad experience with them at The Leaths.

In the afternoon of that same day we looked at Fenwick Jackson's place, an ICI costed farm. He was a silage fattener, as we were, but who had introduced the system first - he or I - we never quite established. There nothing but Friesians were used. Big cattle, and very good cattle at that, were produced, and they sold extremely well. He stocked them well too. He and I were showing roughly the same gross margin; the only advantage I had was that I sold the cattle at a lighter weight because the Friesians took longer to fatten, and that cost more money. That afternoon there was much with which to make comparisons.

The next farm we visited had just opened up a new beef unit. There was a big rectangular building, and all the cattle were bedded from straw elevators just under the roof. Obviously it was a very expensive shed, and many people were of the opinion that it had cost far too much, but it worked, and it looked tremendous. I was quite impressed, but there was much criticism amongst some of the more learned people. When we returned to base we had dinner and a discussion as well as a few drinks, a rather nice way to relax.

These two days had gone well, and on the third and last day I had to make my little speech. This was quite an ordeal because it was a brand-new lecture hall at the University and had gadgets rather like the pre-war cinema organs, which went up and down while being played. There was a huge console with buttons and stops and starters all over the place. It fascinated me because there were microphones here, there and everywhere, and if I ever had a microphone near my face I stuttered, and if I stuttered I had to say a word that began with 'b' and ended with 'r'. To my delight, this had a happy knack of keeping people wide awake. I started playing with these buttons and the blackboard shot up or shot down, and various things went fizzing about, and I was thoroughly enjoying myself while I was delivering what I thought was a serious, well-thought-out and planned paper.

Now, I never did and never could stick to the prepared paper, because if you have a stutter and get stuck with a word, you immediately change it. This used to get the press hopping mad when I went off at a tangent, but the whole thrust of the thing was still the same. My talk was on how you should feed your cattle; how you should start them off as calves; how you should go on to give them the second stage at grass; how you should produce the right sort of silage for the third and final fattening stage; and how The Leaths system worked.

I got along nicely and eventually sat down and waited for question time. I answered several fairly normal questions, until the Irish contingent got going. Just after the war a fellow by the name of Dr Paddy Walsh had gathered around him an Advisory Service of people of the highest calibre. All those whom I had met were extremely bright and knew their subjects exceedingly well. The two whom I knew best of all were Joe Hart and Aidan Conway; they were at the Research Station at The Grange in Meath, not far from Dublin, and they made a wonderful job there with beef. They knew their stuff, and did the lot. There was also a sheep man who ran the Research Station in Galway. He was a clever man and very easy to listen to and understand. The smartest one of them all, I thought, was a man by the name of Brown, who ran the famous dairy unit at Moorpark outside Cork. He was very much a live wire, extremely bright, very amusing, and said exactly what he thought, so on this occasion he and I soon had quite a rapport going. His question to me, however, took me by surprise.

'Mr Maclaren,' he said, 'what is decent silage?'

I said, 'Well, it has a low pH, certainly not more than 4. It has a high dry matter, something between 23, 24 or 25 if you can get it, with a reasonable starch equivalent, and a correspondingly good protein equivalent, which in all produces a jolly good silage.'

He answered me, 'What absolute bloody rubbish. I want a proper analysis of silage.'

I asked, 'What do you mean?'

'Well', he said, 'I want to know about the megajoules and all that sort of thing.'

In all my total ignorance I said that I had never heard of such things. It could have been a Greek word as far as I was concerned, and totally unnecessary. I can assure you it brought about quite a discussion. The repartee amused the audience, and he and I became firm friends after that.

I would advise anybody who wants to know about dairying to go to Moorpark, a place well worth visiting, where they will find the whole thing completely under control. It is in Cork, which is a very favoured area, and the ground is light so stock can be out-wintered. In 1994 they had an Open Day and 10,000 people turned up.

I remember two other occasions that gave me great amusement. One was when I spoke at Perth to a full hall - a completely full hall - at the back of the Station Hotel. The welcome usually received on such an occasion is an immediate ego-booster, and afterwards, when you get the feeling that every word you utter is being listened to, it soars even higher.

I remember with fondness a friend of mind getting up at question time and asking me why a weighbridge was such an important thing on a farm, and could I please tell another story. I explained the importance of weighing beef stock at least every month, and how you kept graphs on the wall, showing the progress made and assisting in decisions as to whether to up this or down that. Making management decisions with the help of a weighbridge was, to my way of thinking, a tremendous asset.

As to his request for another story, I granted quite readily because the art of public speaking is to be able to keep your audience 'alive'. I told the story of the very nervous traveller, the man who was always at the railway station long before the train was due to arrive, or at the airport long before the aeroplane was due to fly. This poor chap had arrived at Dumfries station and had as usual a long time to wait, and did not know what to do with himself. He suddenly saw one of those talking weighing machines, so he thought to himself, 'I'll go and see if this thing is accurate.'

He put in a coin and a voice said, 'You are 6 foot 3 inches, you have brown hair and blue eyes. You weigh 13½ stone and you are catching the 11.20 to King's Cross.' When he heard all this he was positively taken aback, and was sure that there was some collusion between the ticket office and the weighing machine, so he waited a few minutes, went back and repeated the whole performance and was told exactly the same thing.

He was certain then that it was a fix, so he went and asked a porter if he could find him a mailbag, and if he would tie him into the mailbag he would give him 5 shillings. The porter was then to wheel him along, put him on the weighing machine and put the coin in it. This, he was certain, would confuse the issue.

'Certainly, Sir,' said the porter, willing to oblige. He found a mailbag, tied the man in and put him on the weighing machine. The voice said, 'You are 6 foot 3 inches, you have brown hair and blue eyes. You weigh 13½ stone and you are a silly bugger because you have just missed the 11.20 to King's Cross.'

Those sort of stories helped to lighten the proceedings once you got a rapport going, and it was an exhilarating experience.

On another occasion I was speaking at a meeting at an agricultural college outside Salisbury. A day or two before I was due to go down there, there was a fire and the venue had to be changed. We ended up in some school hall. On these occasions I tried to arrive in the area some hours before the meeting, to be able to go around with the ICI people and look at the various farms and systems used. As well as that I liked to talk to the people who knew all about the area, and to meet the chairman and to visit his farm if possible. In other words, I liked to get the feel of the place, and by the evening of the meeting I felt I was 'au fait' with what was happening in the area.

I had to speak first, so I said my little bit about beef, sheep and dairying, then I sat down and the next man stood up and said his bit. When it came to question time there were lots of easy-to-answer questions to start with, then a man in the front row got up and said, 'Mr Maclaren, could you please explain why your figures appear to be much better than everybody else's? I can only imagine that because you belong to ICI you get your fertilisers free and everything else free and that they are not in the costings.'

We were often asked that sort of question, but then he went overboard by asking me if I could tell him what salary ICI paid me for a very ordinary job. I was absolutely incensed, a) that the chairman had allowed such a question to go through, and b) that I was put in the position of having to think up a very quick answer, so I said, 'Yes, but only if you tell me how often you have slept with other women apart from your wife!' Now that caused an absolute uproar - the place was heaving with laughter. I sat down and all went on very quietly after that.

When the meeting was finished, however, the late John Cherrington, who was a friend of mine, and who had previously asked me to write two articles on beef for the *Financial Times*, came up to me and said, 'That was an appalling question to be put. You should have never been asked that, but you do not know just how near the bone your reply was. The guy is a well-known womaniser, and it served him bloody well right.'

The chairman ought to have been hauled over the coals. This awful man had no right to have been chosen in the first place - he was ex-ADAS. On occasions when you think you have blown it and everything seems to be going wrong, it is comforting to hear reassuring words such as those of John Cherrington.

The day after I had spoken somewhere, it was the headlines that I enjoyed, especially the headlines in large type. One classic example was after a talk in which I had said that the haycrop was a disaster if the weather was bad for the next crop. Large headlines reported that an ICI expert had said that the haycrop *was* a disaster. It was not, of course. What I had said had been misquoted, but still there was a certain amusing element.

The other talks I enjoyed doing were related to intensive beef production on grass - 'The Future Looks Bright For Dairy Beef', '£38 Gross Margin From Grass Fed Beef' and 'Beef Production System Which Shows A Profit' are examples of the type of larger and more sober headings.

Other headlines would be something like 'Barley-Beef Blow', or 'It's An I'm Alright Jack Future', which was a heading concocted from comments of mine at a discussion group meeting when I said, 'Unless we look after ourselves, there is no Government who will look after us.' I believed in this statement then, and I still do.

Some especially eye-catching headlines were 'Dramatic Change in the Modern Beef Production' and 'Fast Buck Men Criticised'. This was when a lot of foreign stock was being imported and people were paying enormous prices to bring it into the country, and selling it at even higher prices. Half of them were no damn good. When I was having a go at the banks, 'Chronic Problem of Finding Farming Capital' was the headline that appeared, and many others were similar. The resulting traumas were something you learned to accept.

As soon as I became a consultant I gave up public-speaking, and have kept my mouth tightly shut since. Having said that, I am now retired, and I have just been asked to write another press article that I know will be hard-hitting. I hope this is not to be the 'second round', but even if it is I feel that experience has made me tough enough to cope with the consequences.

8.
NEW LIFE AND CONSULTANCY

The good, the hoppers and the no-hopers

'The effective consultants are the one-man shows. The institutional ones are disastrous. They waste time, cost money, demoralise, distract your best people and do not solve problems. They are people who borrow your watch to tell you what time it is and then walk off with it.'

I saw the above quote in the financial pages of a business paper many years ago, and was delighted when I found it again pasted into my scrapbook. The author is unknown, but if I were to meet him I could back up every word of the truth of it.

When I started my consultancy work I was somewhat anxious about making enough money to afford our new home, Brooklands at Crocketford, west of Dumfries, with its gardener, etc. I had to work out a very careful budget in order to live in the way to which I had become accustomed. The other thing was that I was now self-employed and, in the first year, exempt from Pay As You Earn. This seemed a doddle. I felt as if I was getting rich very quickly, which was not really the case, because from then on the Income Tax demands arrived, which did in fact mean that I had to work even harder to bring in the amount required.

I started with a bank of clients whose land totalled about 50,000 acres. They were scattered all over the place, but I needed more. This was shortly after I had left ICI and two firms were attempting to woo me - a very good feeling. The first was a very well-known firm of Land Agents, so I went to London for an interview, but at the mention of having to work with Tom, Dick and Harry and in Yorkshire or Durham or wherever, I suddenly thought, 'No, not on your life'. I had also taken an instant dislike to two of the people I would have had to work with! The other firm was a large seeds firm. I gave it serious consideration, but in the end I decided to go it on my own and hope for the best.

I had to decide then where I was going to do most of my work and what sort of work I was going to do. I did not want to work with pigs and poultry. It had to be dairying; it had to be hill farming; it had to be sheep; and it had to be suckler cows and beef in various ways and all arable crops. That was all. I was not going to poke my nose into other things about which I knew nothing. It was not very long before I had farms from Caithness down to Cornwall and from Sutherland to the South Coast of England. I was obviously going to have to be very busy to make my business profitable. Without the help of the people to be mentioned later, it might have been fraught with difficulties.

What I looked for in people who approached me to act as their consultant was an instant mutual liking. If that was not the case, then it was a non-starter. If I did like the person and found him to be genuine, and if I had not heard any bad reports about him, then I would ask to see the farm plan, the maps and the accounts for the last two or three years so that I could have a good look at the situation before ever going near the farm itself. If I agreed to take it on, only then would I go to the farm. One thing I pride myself on, and people said that I did it well, is the ability to assess a farm in a very short time - what should be done, why it should be done and when it should be done. That to me was the easy part of it. The more difficult part was to return home and write reports on my findings, make proposals in report form, and hope to goodness that I had got it right.

I have subtitled this book *Sixty Years of Farming, Fun and Frustration*, and the breakdown goes something like this.

Farmers only suffer frustration from three main causes: Weather, Government Policy and Civil Servants.

First, Weather: either too wet or too dry, too cold or too mild, too windy or no wind.

Second, Government Policy: up until 1972 there were governments of every hue and colour and poor or non-existent price reviews. I was on a committee of three that used to go to the Scottish Office every spring and put our case for price rises, etc, a very civilised and sensible way of working as we all knew our subject.

Third, Civil Servants: from 1972 we had the European Economic Community with its great plans and the first Farm & Horticultural Development Scheme (FHDS). These changed things dramatically for many as the banks were willing to back feasibility studies, and considerable sums of money were available over a five-year period. It was the making of many, but also the worst scenario for others. This added an additional 'F word' when dealing with the tangle of red tape and the plethora of civil servants who always seemed hell bent on delaying everything. The final straw to make the 'F word' a common adjective were IACS forms. These were interpreted in different ways in Scotland and England and caused and are still causing far too much hassle and waste of time.

I classified Farmers into three groups: the good; the 'hoppers', changing from one system to another for no better reason than that they had seen their neighbours do it; and the 'no-hopers', who had to be persuaded to pack up.

The following stories are to support the opening quote. On more than one occasion I was called on to clear up the mess made by some of the fashionable firms and saw the cost of their efforts. I was asked by a partner in one firm to meet him in Inverness and go and look at a large estate where money was apparently no object. The plan was to acquire more farmland.

I duly took the guy there. He knew nothing about Scottish farming and we looked at the land in question. I decided that we could do 'a' or 'b' with it, and recommended a price that would make it a good acquisition. I also took him round two other places that I was looking after in the area, and I showed him how it would work. Then I sent him a six-page report. He said that he was delighted and that he would turn it into 30 pages to present to his employers with a 'glossy' costing - no doubt at least five times what I had received for all the information and figures that were produced.

The other case was even worse. The managing agents had allowed a farming enterprise to run up large losses for six years, with the effect that the tax rebate given over that period was not allowable and had to be repaid to the local Inspectors. This did not please the owner and his accountants, or the managing agents, who asked if I could help.

I rang up the three people whose judgement I relied on implicitly. The first was Tony Allen of Champness, later to become Saffery & Champness. He was a brilliant young man with tremendous foresight, and was making his name as the complete expert in estate and land management in the United Kingdom. I worked with him for 27 years and never stopped marvelling at his capacity for work and sound advice.

The other was an ICI colleague who became the Head of the Economics Department at the West of Scotland Agricultural College and did wonders there before he died. He was a wonderful report-writer and knew all about macro and micro economics, which was Greek to me but went down especially well with the Boards of some of the big companies for whom I worked. He always put the summary first, as most Boards could not be bothered to read over 30 or 40 pages of figures. In addition there was one member of his staff who could dissect farm accounts down to the finest detail and was always right. It was, indeed, a formidable team.

I asked Tony Allen what he thought about the tax repayment problem

Myself in about 1965.

The Leaths farmhouse.

The first big Open Day at The Leaths on 18 May 1961, arranged by ICI's associate enterprise, Scottish Agricultural Industries Ltd. Addresses started at 10.30 am and went on until lunchtime, after which the 500 or so visitors were taken on a tour of the farm in 12 SAI lorries, and had a crop and grass demonstration at each site. A break for tea at 3.30 pm was followed by discussion time, finishing at 5.30 pm. It was all highly organised, which made for an extremely good day.

Top Our children David (left), Annie and Hugh in the 1950s.

Middle Shaun (left) and Hugh at The Leaths in the 1960s.

Left Charlie at The Leaths.

Jean and I at Brooklands in 1973, 'tiptoeing through the snowdrops'.

My boss at ICI, Bob Hamilton (left), Senior Vice-Chancellor and Chairman of the Senate of Queen's University, Belfast, receiving a presentation from the Vice-Principal, Sir Gordon Beveridge.

Culfargie farm: the shed for 1,000 ewes at Tarrylaw.

A 24-meter MB self-propelled sprayer and liquid fertiliser applicator.

A view across Culfargie with the farm in the distance.

Annie's wedding at Brooklands, and what a wedding it was! We had a marquee on the lawn in front of the house with a wooden floor, not only for comfort but also so that the boys could invite their friends to an 'all-night' dance. Although it snowed the day before, the day itself was clear, but catering for over 650 guests was quite a task!

Owen's Barn, Folkingham: the spraying aeroplane.

My car and 90 acres of oil-seed rape, with one of the former rocket sites in the background. A swathe was cut in the OSR so that the plane could land on the perimeter track.

A self-propelled oil-seed rape swather at Folkingham.

Oil-seed rape going into an on-the-floor dryer.

We had to drain the whole farm; here, tile draining is in progress.

A Simba subsoiler behind a DH4 Crawler.

Brooklands: the house and (*below*) the Lodge.

The pond at Brooklands. Ernest Binks, our invaluable gardener, encouraged us to renovate the pond and stock it with trout, plant trees, enlarge the woods and really try to look after the place as it deserved.

Part of the rose border in the walled garden. We doubled the garden in size, and planted more good large-leaved rhododendrons and other trees until we had 1½ acres of walled garden and an additional 6 acres of kept borders full of rich and rare plants, as well as a large area of grass to cut. It was a wonderful way to relax at weekends and whenever I was at home.

The leaf corner in the walled garden, with Jean and a friend sheltering under a natural umbrella! Jean is artistic and was obviously as keen as me to have the garden looking well. Without her we should have been lost, as her artistic eye kept the planting of all things just right. We never planted without first seeking approval from the 'planning officer', as we called her.

Brooklands from the south-east on 18 May 1992, from the cover of the brochure we produced when regretfully we sold the house. Brooklands was a truly lovely place, a light, airy 19th-century house with marvellous views and lovely grounds.

Our grandchildren racing on the tennis court at Brooklands.

Glenfarg Ripple, the best dog I ever owned.

I had. He told me the name of the Inspector and said 'Have a go', but he was doubtful if I could win. Having been subjected to an MI5 type of scrutiny, I was given the go ahead. I waited for a spell of good weather and went to have a look. It was a complete mess. After discussing it with the great farm account dissector, we decided to tell the truth and explain that if they had sold the Galloway cattle at Castle Douglas, the Blackface sheep at Oban and the Cheviots at Inverness, the last year would have been profitable. It was accepted and they got £60,000 back. I got £1,000 to cover all my work and expenses, and not even a bloody 'thank you'. That hurt.

Tony and I had one great triumph. We were having our dram at Brooklands and I said that it was very unfair that the 50-odd acres of grass parks around our new home was taxed as unearned income. Tony asked me what I did to earn it, and I told him that I had to plough the fields, work them down and sow grass as well as having to put on 2 tons of magnesium limestone, 10 cwt of triple phosphate and enough nitrogen to make it all grow. We also looked at the stock daily and had to fence the sides of the woods and spray out all the chickweed and thistles that appeared. Tony said that there was a case and wrote to the Inspector of Taxes. The answered with, 'Dear Mr Allen, I am beguiled with your argument and will certainly allow earned income relief.' We won a famous victory. From then on all grass parks were treated as earned income, which was only fair.

Most, if not all, Tax Inspectors were wary of Tony, as he knew their job better than they did. Sadly he died aged only 55 and is missed by so many people. His counsel was always right, he was a great friend and helped me enormously. I miss him.

I did a job while I was with ICI for the late Duke of Norfolk. The job was up here in Scotland, on a part of the land that he had at Caerlaverock. It was to do with goose damage, and he was extremely grateful. I had never met him, but he did invite me down to a two-day event at Arundel run by one of the newspapers and ICI. Lots of important people, including the new Chairman of ICI, were there, and everyone assembled on the gorgeous cricket field - quite impressive. Identity badges were worn, and whether the Duke did it on purpose or not I do not know, but my designation was 'Peter Maclaren, ICI Scotland'. You can imagine a lot of the ICI people saying, 'Who the hell does this fellow think he is?' I enjoyed wearing it, and still have it.

My 'empire' eventually went further - I cannot remember how many thousand acres. I even worked in Iran for a short time before the Shah was deposed, and in Natal in South Africa. I thought that to be a wonderful country and frightfully exciting work could be done there. One of the most interesting jobs that I ever did was on an island. I was met off the ferry by the chap who was to take me to the estate and show me around. Not long after we met he produced an envelope for me and in it was a letter from the owner of the estate asking me to report on the staff, the plan and the farm manager, and could I get one and soon? It was quite unusual, for I had done my homework, but I had not expected to be asked to report on the men.

Having spent a day and a night there I arrived home in Scotland pretty tired from the journey. I went to bed, but at about 11.30 I was disturbed by the telephone ringing. It was the private secretary to this tycoon estate owner, and this very charming voice said that 'Mr Snooks' was coming up to Scotland and would be in Dumfries the following night and could I give him my report then? Also, he said, he would like me to dine with him and discuss various things. My reports were always drafted first in longhand, chopped around and finally given to my secretary to process. I had not even started on 'Mr Snooks's' report. I said that I would do what I could.

I duly met him in Dumfries for dinner and we had a thorough discussion. He then opened my report and went straight to the back page, which was the one on staff, and said that he would deal with it in the morning. And so he did. That was the fastest report I was ever called to make and, quite amazingly, action on it was also taken literally within the day.

A lot of my work was in the north, Ross-shire and Inverness-shire. I actually started two big suckler herd cattle groups with three farmers involved in each of them. One was called Ross Roxburgh (it was in Ross-shire and Roxburghshire), and the other was the Black Isle Group. These consisted between them of well over 1,000 cows, all bulled by Angus bulls in those days; the various other breeds came later on. It was important for farmers in those days to get their houses in order - to get into the spirit of co-operation - but they not too keen to do this. They wanted to remain individuals, to be independent and not to feel the need to join up with anyone else or to work in groups. Now we know better - farmers are beginning to think on a much bigger scale, nationally and individually. As far as the two groups were concerned I literally ran them, managed them, and even paid their accounts and much more. It was quite hard going to get all the people concerned to do exactly what you expected from them at the time, and required a lot of attention.

I had learned about suckler cows earlier and I was absolutely certain that we must have them spring calving in one group and late summer calving on the other so that we could have a continual flow of calves for the groups and a steady flow for fattening in Roxburghshire. This was in my pioneering days, so I reckon I was the instigator of the autumn and spring calving programme.

After about three years things turned somewhat sour; all grant sources became exhausted, the farmers started squabbling amongst themselves and eventually the group broke up. It was a pity in one way, but perhaps sensible in another. They continued to run their suckler cows, but obviously did not want the hassle of working together. It was a salutary lesson to me and one that I have not forgotten.

The Iran job was tremendous. It was a big outfit, at that time selling Friesian heifers to important people in Iran. We were talking about herds of thousands of cows and so on - quite extraordinary. There was irrigation, of course, enabling enormous crops of lucerne to be grown, up to 14 a year. In the hills beyond Teheran were ancient storage tanks for millions and millions of gallons of water; they had to be big enough to cope with the melting snow in the summer. There was water everywhere, and although the ground was dirt, not very good, with that amount of water, heat and fertiliser you could make anything grow.

The exciting thing for me was that I had been asked to start up an advisory service for the north of Teheran - in other words from Teheran to the Caspian Sea, a mere 1,000 miles by air - and this was to be my 'patch'. I looked around for someone who was highly qualified in all these things, and I could not find anyone better qualified and more suitable than Professor Mac Cooper. Just come back from Spain and at a loose end, he thought it was a 'bloody good idea', and that we could make a hatful of money. It all looked terrific on paper - Mac Cooper with 27 letters after his name and me with a lesser number - all very impressive and confidence-inspiring. I have no doubt that we would have proved a good investment, but the Shah had been deposed so we never really got off the ground or were put to the test. However, it was all very interesting and exciting for a short time.

The first time I went out there we flew to Beirut, the last British Airways aeroplane to fly in before the troubles started. The place was virtually on fire and the stewardess warned that we would be boarded by guerrillas. We were told to try to hide anything valuable as best we could, and sure enough, when we landed, well away from the terminal buildings, the doors were opened and these bandits came aboard with guns slung over their necks. They asked who we were and what was our business, but were obviously reasonably satisfied, so all was well, but it was rather unnerving.

The South African job was great fun. I already worked in the North of Scotland for the people who owned the vast 15,000-acre estate, where I spent a week. It went up to 7,000 feet and had a huge irrigation system, enabling them to grow over 200 acres of potatoes, a lot of maize, a crop of which I had very little experience, and lots of vegetables. The nearest large market town was Durban, along some 150 miles of roads that were not always good.

The potato crop was liable to be battered by hailstones during the summer because it was high in the Drakensburgh Hills, but strangely enough, apart from the hailstones, the worst pests, which I had certainly never encountered before, were porcupines. When the veldt was ploughed up and the potatoes planted, a wire fence had to be erected in order to keep the porcupines out, otherwise they would have dug out the lot.

The potatoes were all seed potatoes and graded by size. It was difficult to get the machinery for this purpose, but there were a tremendous number of people hanging around. I discovered later that this particular farm employed more than 60 people, and their families were with them. Houses and schools had to be built for them, and a schoolmaster had to be found; thus evolved a sizeable community, all on its own. There was also a lot of stock. One of the men was an excellent stockman, and we got the suckler cow system going - they were Shorthorn crosses, Limousines, etc.

The flora and fauna were wonderful, and the birds quite incredible. Britain has just over 300 species compared with South Africa's 900, and it was wonderful to see all of this. Vast irrigation lakes were stocked and the rainbow trout were bigger than I had ever seen before. I used to spend about an hour in the evening at the lake, when I could cast a salmon fly in the water and out would come a rainbow weighing seven to eight pounds. It was a holiday as well as business.

A few years later, however, I was telephoned in a panic and asked if I could possibly get on the next aeroplane. There was not enough money to pay the wages for that week, they could not get any more money out of England, and they had to do cash flows while I was there, get them to the accountant by Thursday morning and take them to the bank in Pietermaritzburg on the Friday, before I returned home on the Saturday having sorted everything out.

The aeroplane on which I was to travel kept 'playing up', causing delays, so I was a day late, arriving on the Tuesday. After a quick look around the farm I had to sit down in a poky little room and work out the cash flow and what exactly was to happen. By the greatest of luck all went well. I took the relevant papers to the accountant, who seemed pleased with them, then to the bank manager who gave us the money. We could now pay the men and that brought about a sigh of relief. It meant that there had been very big concessions made on the part of the owner, so I produced a plan that recommended that three of the four managers who looked after the place should be sacked. This was done the next day, and we left it in the hands of one man who made an excellent job of looking after the stock. Within three years of this trip the farm was thriving and this same man, accompanied by his wife and family, was able to make a trip to Scotland and to stay with us. He was a delighted and happy man, but it had been damned hard work in South Africa in the first place and I would never wish to mount an operation of the same type again. It was, however, a tremendous experience, although fraught with difficulties.

In the 26 years of consultancy I did my travelling by car, except on some occasions. My journeys to Islay were always by plane, and I generally flew when I was going to Exeter. I started off with a Volvo estate and I did 30-35,000 miles every year. I was on my sixth Volvo when Tony Allen said, 'You know, Peter, it is time you bought yourself a decent car.'

I wanted to know what was wrong with my Volvo - it was fast and it was big.

'I think you should have a Mercedes,' he said.

Little did he know that I had a secret passion for a Mercedes. I thought it might buck up my morale if I thought people were saying, 'What an important consultant he must be when he can afford to drive around in a car like that.' I leased my first and my instructions from Tony were to run it round the clock. Unfortunately, however, I did not see a sample of the colour before it arrived; on the chart it was 'Cayenne', so I thought it would be a good orangy colour and, with black upholstery, would look quite smart. When it did arrive I was very impressed with the running side of it, but the colour. . . It was horrific, to say the least. When one of my clients saw it he said, 'That is a very smart car, Peter, but, my God, I do not like "teat pink" cars!' That was enough. I had to change it instantly.

I changed it for a Mercedes 280 estate, and in a very short time I had registered 130,000 miles. It gave me no trouble at all and I ran it until the rubber of the windows started to perish. As I was shooting less and did not have to carry the dogs around as much, I changed to a Mercedes 280 saloon.

In total I had six Volvos and five Mercedes, which includes the one I have now - a 230TE estate - as I found it easier for suitcases and I also knew that it would be more suitable for transporting plants when flitting time came. All the time I had absolutely no trouble with either make of car; they were all purchased from Patons of Carlisle who are the agents for both and whose attention to customer service is spot on. Any time that my car was in for service or required any major surgery, they lent me another one free. It was and still is a very happy relationship.

We have been fortunate and can claim to have had only one smash. We were driving a Mercedes on a trip to Lincolnshire and had stopped at a pub for lunch and to change drivers, or better still to allow me to have a couple of gin and tonics. Jean took over and was doing fine until she came up to traffic lights at some road works. She duly stopped behind the car in front, but then had the whole back pushed in by a bloody fool in a Volvo. My son Hugh was in the back and behind him were the two dogs and our guns. There was glass everywhere, but by sheer good luck the dogs and guns were all right.

We got back on the road. It was rather a still kind of day and we went down with all the exhaust fumes pouring in. It was dark by the time we reached our destination, having witnessed a most horrific accident on the old A1 near Newark, requiring us to go on the side roads, still with the fumes gassing us. The car took a month to repair, but Patons loaned me another and I got on with my work.

9.
CULFARGIE AND
A WEDDING

Cereals, loaves and fishes

Part of the fun of being a wandering consultant was that if you were asked to do a job a long way away, you quite often stayed with the people. If you arrived in the morning you were generally treated hospitably and given a cup of coffee. If you arrived in the evening you were treated sensibly and offered a dram - very civilised.

The one host I remember most vividly to this day was a terribly nice and kind young man who was having trouble with his farming. He was very keen to make a great success of it, and asked me to come and stay. I arrived at about 6.30 in the evening; his mother was there and he very courteously asked me if I would like a drink. I replied, 'Yes, I would love a whisky and water please.' The three of us sat down and chatted about farming and so on. However, having taken my first sip, I put it down very quickly, then was conscious of him keeping an eye on me until he eventually said, 'Is there anything wrong with your drink, Mr Maclaren?'

I said, 'Well I am afraid, yes, it is sherry and water'.

I have never forgotten the expression on his face. The poor chap was so embarrassed, but he did laugh, which was great.

The next day we went round the farm. I made notes as we went and as I kept coming on barley fields that had been undersown, I wrote in my book, 'Field number whatever, barley US'. At one stage he became frightfully agitated and said, 'What do you mean? My barley is not useless at all!' Naturally this gave us another laugh when it was explained. He went on from there and has done jolly well ever since.

A very different type of farm in Perthshire, and one that was in a pretty bad way, was run by a Board and known as Culfargie Farms. Culfargie was farmed by a manager, and at the time I was called in drastic surgery was obviously an immediate requirement, and my report was to that effect. A drier of their own was a must as all the grain was taken down off the combines in little coup-carts to a drying place just outside Perth. The combines were either stopped or produced very little output while working in this fashion.

The whole system was a disaster - oats and a year's grass, then the following spring it was grazed by lambs, then it was potatoes or swedes, then it was back to oats or barley. The yields were appalling, the crops were late, and the grain just did not pay. There was no proper handling or storage for the swedes or potatoes, and the good years were gone. It was difficult to make any money out of seed potatoes.

What then happened was that swedes and potatoes were abandoned, and the acreage was used to let: over 200 acres for over £200 per acre. This way we got an early entry into wheat. As the potato situation worsened, the quota was sold for over £90,000, and the acreage that was let was split into land for potatoes and vining peas. It all went extremely well.

My reasons for taking this course of action was quite simple - there was no storage. To put up one of those new environment-controlled buildings with a proper grading line would have cost the earth. In my opinion the money would be better spent putting up a grain drier costing much less. It made the farm very much more viable.

The Board agreed and accepted the report. For a year the manager tried hard, but he never got anywhere. Unhappily, eventually I had to say, 'It is no good. Nothing will ever happen while you have this old farm manager.' He was therefore pensioned off and a young man engaged in his place. I could not advertise in the English papers because of an on-going strike, so I advertised in the Scottish papers. There were only 17 applicants and of those only one looked as if it might be any good. This was a young man who had come up from the south where he had been an ADAS Advisor. He was a lad who had a very good head on him and had the reputation of being a very hard worker. He was a friend of two of my sons and they assured me that he was a first-class chap, so I told the Board and that is how he came to be engaged at Culfargie. He is still there, 14 years on. Brian Kaye is this young man's name, and when he came to Scotland to work it was for a friend on an arable farm not very far from where he is now. He was to stay there only until the son of the owner returned from the Army, which he did, so I did not steal anybody else's farm manager.

Brian was to be in charge of the 800-acre farm, which included some hill land, but while he was on his honeymoon two other farms right opposite came on the market - one good, one not so good. They were bought so that when he came back a week or ten days later he found himself manager of double the acreage. Within a couple of years another 200 acres were bought, so in total he was farming some 1,600 acres, including all his hill land. On this additional 200 acres the sheds were not in good condition, so they were altered and turned into a bull-fattening unit. The calves were left entire from the spring and autumn calving herd, and were fed on the cheapest rations possible, and this paid off handsomely.

My advice at the time - 1981 - was that instead of having all this spring corn, which meant that everything was late and you got nothing done, there should be a change-over to growing winter barley, oil-seed rape and winter wheat; also that as much as possible of the cereals acreage should be sown in the autumn, but that a good acreage of spring barley should still be kept. This was done and it was hoped that the marketing would be right.

There were too many men on the place. There were too many wheelbarrows on the place. There were wheelbarrows to take the muck out of the sheds, and in one shed alone there were five. There were wheelbarrows for all the jobs. Some of these wheelbarrows had to go, and some of the men had to go too. We increased the livestock so that eventually there was a suckler herd of 100 and a shed was built for in-wintering. The calves were kept and sold in the spring. In other words, the system was reversed, and it proved very successful.

There was a Blackface ewe flock on the hill that lambed 130 per cent one year. However, we knew that the reclaimed land on the hill could be worked to greater advantage, so in 1985, which was the most ghastly harvest that Scotland had ever had, we started talking about a sheep shed costing some £50,000, but which should eventually pay off. (My second son had one where he worked - good recommendation.) The dreadful harvest meant that every acre of grain had lost about £100, and unfortunately there was not enough free capital to build the shed, so it was some four years before the sheep shed went up. It still stands, however, and holds over 1,000 ewes.

The lambing percentage in 1994 went up to 203 per cent, though lambing takes a lot of managing and a lot of men - three people per shift. We also fattened cattle as well as lambs.

At the time of the change-over to cereal-growing we had to put up a grain-drier. The Board was very understanding. Generally when I put a good case forward it was favourably received, so we were able to buy a drier with enough wet grain storage to keep things going. It has certainly proved its worth. The machinery at Culfargie has always been of the best, and has brought out the full capacity of the land, and of the men as well.

About seven years ago the 'one-pass' system was started, certainly the first in Perthshire. In short, it means that as soon as the winter barley is harvested in early August, you go straight in with a plough. The plough has a press behind it and in between the tractor wheels, and that is followed directly with a drill and rotary harrow. Therefore while the harvest is going on, two men are sowing behind them. This saves a tremendous amount of time and ensures that crops are on time and, therefore, produce good yields.

There has been oil-seed rape on the farm since before the 'double zeros' arrived, producing over 2 tons an acre. A consistent 4 tons per acre of wheat is produced, and winter barley exceeds 3½ tons. It is a very successful and profitable set-up.

As well as the low-ground farms, there are two large hill farms quite a long way off, and these have two main hirsels* of sheep; there were three originally, but we turned them into two of 1,000 ewes each. There are 100 spring-calving cows that are wintered on the low ground farms on pot-ale and straw. The whole system knits very well.

During this time we became environmentally conscious - I think that is the right phrase - so we repaired or put in new hedges. Dual-purpose woods were planted to act as shelter belts and for shooting purposes; grants were and are still available. However, we tried to look after the countryside as it should be. Many farmers at that time, unfortunately, forgot that. Environmentally we were friendly, but farming-wise we were efficient. It was an excellent lesson for a lot of people. Unhappily I have had to give it all up as I have been told to take things easy - quite a bore! I really did enjoy the challenge as well as working along with Brian Kaye.

One of the big jobs you find yourself landed with if you are looking after a lot of land is head-hunting. A good farm manager is priceless. I have done a lot of this in my time, and found it strangely difficult to get some employers to understand the intricacies of the operation. Not only is finding the right person for the situation important, but keeping a guiding interest for a period of at least three years is also a must. I have had the experience of engaging a farm manager, leaving him to get on with the job, then finding the place in a hell of a mess and having to start all over again, simply because the owner was not prepared to pay my fee to keep an eye on the place. My fee was never all that much - at least I didn't think so - but certainly worth it to avoid such a situation. It is easy enough to fire people, but it is not much fun getting a reputation, and have them think, 'Oh, my God, here is Maclaren again. That means I am going to get my books.' I avoided that if possible.

Jean and I had two boys, then a girl, then another two boys. Like all children, they were all very different until they grew up. The eldest son, David, is a physiotherapist and lives in the Vale of Belvoir. He works locally but does two days a week in London; he also gardens and keeps bees. Our second son, Hugh, is a farm manager for a large Perthshire estate. He does an excellent job and has been there for over 20 years. He also looks after a marvellous sporting estate passed on to him and his brothers by their aunt some years ago.

* A hirsel is a cut or small number of sheep - 40-50 - on hill land, which stay in around the same area and are self-contained.

Shaun, our third son, joined the Army and retired recently, after having done 22 years' service, including soldiering in Oman for 12 years. He likes the wide open spaces where he can shoot and fish. He has now gone to a civilian job in New Zealand where, sadly, there is no grouse! The youngest, Charlie, is a trained agriculturalist. He has had many good jobs - farm managing, running a long-distance haulage business and now with an animal feeds firm. Annie, our only daughter, trained as a Cordon Bleu cook. She had her own kitchen for a year or two with Cordon Bleu, then went to America to work and play. For a while on her return she cooked for several prestige firms in London, but being of an adventurous nature she bought a car and became a 'cook-on-wheels' for anyone in the South who wanted a professional cook for special occasions.

She then became engaged to and married a local landowner. What a wedding that was! Annie knew many people and she wanted them all to be there. We decided that the best plan was to have a marquee on the lawn in front of the house with a wooden floor, not only for comfort but also so that the boys could invite their friends to an 'all-night' dance.

A grand total of 670 invitations were sent out, but we fully expected that only around 400 would be able to accept. As the wedding was in March we thought the weather might be a drawback; it actually snowed the day before. To our amazement, however, only 13 people could not make it. The feeding and drinking logistics went out the window, and everything had to be drastically changed, even to the seating in the chapel.

Just to add a bit of spice to the already pickled situation, Jean and I went to South Africa - me to work for a client and then the two of us to have a break - before the big day. We returned ten days before the wedding and immediately I had to go away to visit another client. Everyone thought we were crazy, of course, and expected the equivalent of The Mad Hatter's Tea Party.

Not a bit of it. The snow miraculously disappeared to reveal carpets of snowdrops. The ground was hard enough to take the cars. Everyone was in a jolly mood. Even my late mother-in-law, who was then in her late 80s, was affected; when she saw me dressed up prior to leaving with Annie for the church, she enquired as to whom I was to marry. When I replied that I was married, she promptly replied, 'Oh well, then you must be getting divorced.' She was a great character.

The bride and groom left by car to travel to the nearest airstrip where there was an aeroplane waiting to take them to London on the first stage of their honeymoon trip to Kenya. The plane flew over Brooklands half an hour or so later, leaving Annie's lurcher howling its head off on the front door step. From above she threw down her bouquet and, being a good shot like her father, it landed on the AA man's head.

By now we were somewhat wilted, so we retired for a break before the start of the next part of the programme. What a relief to take off my stiff collar, open the cuffs of my shirt and sink back into my favourite chair to smoke a cigar. It was only for a short time, however, for I had now to dress for dinner. I picked up the ashtray to throw the ash into the fire, but ash, ashtray and cuff links all went in. They were special cuffs given to me by Jean's aunt, one engraved 'Jean', the other 'Peter'. I did manage to salvage one and have had a replacement made for the other.

The young ones and their guests, who had arrived at about 10.00 pm in the evening, enjoyed the dancing until 6.00 in the morning. It was declared by all to have been a great success. My second son was seen dancing to the last waltz with his dog Tara, an enormous deerhound. How wonderful for the young, and how wonderful it was to be oblivious to the din of the young!

10.
CONSERVATION

Iniquity, inequality and inequilibrium

While I was still with ICI in Castle Douglas I was asked to look at goose damage on a farm belonging to a Solway Firth estate. The tenant was the only one of 28 who had been complaining about damage to his grassland from barnacle, greylag and pinkfoot geese, and he said that the rent for the farm, 600 acres with 1,000 acres of merse* for free, was too high. I went along, had a look, and talked to the other 27 tenants who had no complaints. I wrote a report recommending a rent rise as the goose damage was minimal. This was turned down flat by the tenant, so we went to arbitration.

Because the barnacle geese fed almost exclusively on the merse, their droppings were brown, while the grey geese produced green and white ones. The barnacle geese hardly visited the arable areas at all, as their numbers were down to about 600, and strangely enough they left the Solway on about 20 February and flew across to the Rockcliffe marshes in Cumbria until they migrated back to Spitzbergen to breed.

The arbitration was a stern affair with witnesses for both the landlord and the tenant. When it was all over the adjudicator said he would return on such and such a date with his verdict. We all went back on the appointed day to hear that the rent was to rise to £11,000 and if there were any more complaints about the goose damage a further £1,000 would be added.

Five years later the Nature Conservancy Council were told that the tenant was appealing, so I was asked again to report on the damage. In those halcyon days from 1953 to 1961, the NCC had Sir Arthur Duncan as its Chairman. Arthur was a good friend of mine and a marvellous shot, and he always asked me to shoot with him. We had many marvellous days.

* Low, flat marshland.

Sir Arthur was a Cambridge-trained entomologist and lepidopterist, and was a keen and very knowledgeable ornithologist; to my mind he was the complete countryman. He was followed by another professionally trained man, Dr Joe Eggeling, and it was to him that I had to report on this occasion. Both Sir Arthur and Doctor Joe were doubtful if I could win again, as I thought that the rent should include the 1,000 acres of merse, which provided useful grazing except during high tides. Similar merse grazing was commanding £40 per head of cattle on the Rockcliffe marshes, so my recommendation was for a rent of £21,000. It was doom and gloom for some days, but then happily the tenant surrendered and we had won again. The farm is now the centre of the Wetland Trust, and barnacle geese numbers have risen to 13,000.

I would like to think that all the conservation groups, of which there is a plethora, were as effective as the NCC, but unhappily they are not. The Countryside Commission for England and Scotland is good, but the Council for the Protection of Rural England (CPRE) has just launched 'Leisure Landscapes' and forecasts millions of leisure visits to certain areas. I ask, 'Who are the visitors?' If they are the average townsfolk, we do not want them - they are generally more trouble than they are worth and I have learned that they may well be given a very biased anti-farming view. One well-known and respected countryman said that CPRE stood for the 'Council for the Paralysis of Rural England' and thought it very apt.

I put such individuals in the same category as those people fortunate enough to buy a country cottage where they expect everything to be the same as when they bought it, with cattle lying around in fields, but if they as much as smell slurry or silage effluent they rush off to the nearest Environmental Officer to complain. It happened to us in Lincolnshire when we emptied the bull slurry and the Council warned us that they would prosecute if it happened again.

The farm and wildlife groups are good, but in my opinion very few of the others make any sense at all. The trouble is that so many are now 'quangos' made up of people who know damn all about the countryside, and float about making a lot of noise and talking and writing rubbish!

The RSPB certainly restored avocets to their homeland, but I feel that they have now lost their sense of proportion, and should change the 'B' to 'R' for Raptors! Even ardent conservationists are moaning about the present numbers of sparrowhawks, and I read that 8.4 million birds were eaten by them in 1993. Their benefactors are at the same time complaining that our songbirds are getting less. Raptor protection and cat ownership mean that if this goes on there will be no birds left to sing.

I am fully aware that there was a serious decline in raptor numbers and that the chemicals Aldrin and Dieldrin were the main culprits, but when they were banned the eggs were once again fertile and numbers escalated. The explosion in magpies and both hoodie and carrion crows is also alarming, as they are egg and fledgling eaters. Are conservationists totally blinkered to the facts of life?

The EU and our own Government still give generous grants for the regeneration of heather and the extensification of sheep farming, as we are only 84 per cent self-sufficient in lamb and mutton. The situation can only deteriorate and our balance of payments will suffer while the raptors kill off the grouse and nothing eats the heather except the larvae of the emperor moth.

We have only two unique indigenous British birds, the St Kilda wren, found only on St Kilda, and the red grouse, bringing in millions of pounds to the economy and employing labour to look after them as well as having a capital value of £2-4,000 per brace. We are told that hen harriers only take one red grouse chick a day to feed their families. That is absolute drivel. A keeper told me that he saw four chicks taken from one covey in an hour. I know of good grouse moors all over Scotland where more than half the breeding stock are killed by raptors every winter. I was on a moor two years ago on a fine October afternoon and never even heard a cock grouse, when they should all have been proclaiming their territories for all to hear. What are the conservationists thinking about? They really ought to issue licences to accredited owners to restrict the raptors. It is done with the saw-billed duck to preserve the salmon and sea trout parr.

Surely it would be sensible to bring the balance of nature back to *normality*? The Wildlife & Countryside Bill of 1981 has been an unmitigated disaster, and it is time the country people rose up and objected until significant change is achieved. Normality is simple. It means keeping the numbers of all species in the proper proportion. It does not mean going back to the old days when it was thought that everything with a hooked bill must be destroyed. This normality would not need an extra army of civil servants to administer it, but a voluntary board of dedicated countrymen who would advise the Government what steps should be taken to return to the proper balance. The only danger is that we true countrymen are now an endangered species ourselves!

I was amazed to hear recently on an early morning farming radio programme that a new alliance was being formed between the environmentalists and the farmers. I though we had enough groups of this kind already, but not a bit of it. Apparently the Gay Hussar Group was formed when Mr Charles Clover decided to give a dinner party for environmentalists in the Gay Hussar restaurant. Jonathon Porritt, Britain's most prominent 'green', met up with Oliver Walston, a farmer of no mean repute who is totally anti-green. Professor Frank Raymond, who had been Scientific Advisor to the Ministry of Agriculture and whom I knew quite well, had been enlisted as a referee lest the occasion should become somewhat riotous. Much to everyone's astonishment, the evening went remarkably well and, to quote Mr Clover, 'Porritt and Walston turned the evening into an "embarrassing reasonableness"'.

The purpose of the meeting was to discuss the iniquities of paying farmers for land 'set-aside', and also the arable-aid acreage payments. The two sides agreed, quite rightly, that environmentalists and farmers should talk to each other, although I thought we had been doing that for a long time! Another prominent 'green' who was present was Hugh Rave, Director of SAFE Alliance, the new organisation for the farming, environment and safe-food group.

Apparently Walston and Porritt 'reached a symbolic agreement' that the present form of the CAP, not just set-aside, was a disgrace. In a post-GATT world it was absurd to pay farmers production subsidies to grow more of crops that were already in surplus, and then to hand them more money to produce nothing on a proportion of their land. Farmers should be paid instead for things the market did not provide, and that people actually wanted, such as hedges, meadows, woods, skylarks and dry stone walls. The whole country should be an environmentally sensitive area. Set-aside should be abolished. The list of demands forms the substance of the Gay Hussar Group's agenda launched by Porritt at a SAFE Alliance press conference at the Royal Show in 1994.

We have all known for quite some time that set-aside is immoral. We have all known that it should be used for other crops. We have all talked about it. We could produce bio-mass, we could produce poplars, willows and lupins. We could produce oil-seed rape. But we already have LEAF, a group started a few years ago by David Richardson, which seems to me to make a lot more sense than most others. LEAF stands for Linking Environment And Farming, so why do we need yet another?

There are lots of other things that people have been thinking about, and not just today. To introduce another group would simply mean more money to pay expenses and salaries to the people who run it. It seems to me to be as absolutely ridiculous as the word they use for agriculture - 'sustainability'.

'What in the name of heaven is "sustainability"?' you may ask. We all do everything that we can to make farming pay, and those of us who live in the country try to look after it to the best of our ability. What we are in need of now is the common sense approach, for common sense at the end of the day is what most farmers understand. They do not want the countryside to suffer. They have looked after it for hundreds of years. On the other hand, they cannot be expected to farm without reasonable guarantees. All these wonderful new societies do not guarantee them anything. They are simply 'talking-shops', and if they talk long enough the Government of the day, whether it be pink, blue, white or whatever, will respond, they hope.

I feel, partly with tongue in cheek, that we should have a new group of quite another sort. It should be called the BFTF - Be Fair To Farmers. I will be Chairman, and I will not expect to get paid for it. I will gather round me the most wonderful collection of people who will uphold our beliefs in the most forthright manner at the right time. It will be insisted upon that BFTF will be a frightfully upright organisation, and with me as Chairman we are bound to have a lot of fun, and I will not stand for any frustrations!

11.
ISLAY

Rosy Pastor and Ginger Tom

In 1966 I was asked if I would show a well-managed, heavily stocked farm to a young man who had just been appointed as Factor to Islay Estates. He was to have a 'crash course' in farm management with special emphasis on the production of good grass. It was a great success and he has called me 'Super Grass' ever since. The outcome of his visit was that within a year I received a letter from him asking for help as one farm was having a brucellosis storm.

It was the most extraordinary case. There were two suckler cow herds of 100 each; one was housed and the other was wintered out on 'The Warren'. The Warren was the most perfectly sheltered area of over 200 acres of pure sand. The one staff served both farms, although they were about a mile apart. Only the out-wintered cows were aborting. I could not do very much to help except to sympathise and see that every precaution was taken to keep the stock segregated.

Islay is the most beautiful island imaginable. It has a population of about 3,500, and the people are charming. It has about eight distilleries so there is no shortage of whisky and the drams are pretty generous! One has to be careful. . . I remember going out after a splendid dinner, after midnight in June, and being shown part of the island, covered with deer and all in wonderful condition. It never gets fully dark during high summer.

I went over again the following February, and I was amazed to see how little grass there was until I saw all the geese - about 18,000 barnacles and greenland whitefronts. What fascinated me was that in a field near the main road there was a dead goose, and when I went up to it I found the grass nearby grazed absolutely bare, but the grass surrounding the bird was 3-4 inches tall. I had used cages at The Leaths to measure grass growth, so

I suggested we did the same on part of Islay House Farm. The results were quite staggering. There was grazing grass, but it could have been winter barley, growing away like crazy at the beginning of February.

The wildfowl trust had an expert goose-counter who was only too willing to provide me with the numbers of geese over the last 18 years, and it was from his records that the explosion in numbers could be seen only too clearly.

One of the Islay farmers was a wonderful man called Tom Epps. He was the subject of an article in the *Sunday Times* some time ago, and was, I believe, a barrow-boy in London who got fed up and wanted to farm. He and his brothers took a farm on the mainland to gain experience, but after a while they split up and Tom got the tenancy of a farm on Islay by Loch Gruinard - Aarodh Farm.

He set to and built all the buildings required himself. He put on a large dairy, having first visited The Leaths to see our layout. At the same time he was reclaiming the Gruinard flats, which flooded badly. The estate fixed the sea wall and he put in open ditches, just like Holland, and reseeded a large area. He built silage pits and fed draff*, which in those days was free for the carting away. Not content with that, he took on more farms until he farmed all the low ground right along to the end of the loch. The end part was 'The Warren', and there he had some 400 suckler cows that were fed silage and draff. He was a very large and successful farmer.

By re-seeding and draining the land near his dairy farm he immediately improved the feeding for the geese, and the numbers rose quite dramatically to around 25,000. They bred in Greenland and were not the same as Caerlaverock geese, which take the easterly route from Spitzbergen. They were shot in those days and farmers could keep them off their crops, but still numbers rose.

Tom Epps, apart from farming, became a full-time - and big-time - lobsterfisher. He had two boats, fully equipped with radar, etc, and used to go miles out to sea. He made his own creels and used 160 per boat in a long line. Lobsters were cheap in August and September, so he built one and then another holding area, fed by the sea, holding up to half a million lobsters, which were flown out to France. He was a marvellous man who always sent me home with a box of lobsters.

When he retired the farms were sold. Unfortunately they were sold to the Royal Society for the Protection of Birds, and then the trouble started. The dairy was sold off, and consequently the ideal goose grazing was lost and the geese, now protected, looked for pastures new.

Now enter the NCC. Why was there no consultation with the locals

---

* A by-product of whisky distilling and brewing, draff is either wet or dry malting barleys, grain maize or wheat. Normally costing £25 or £30 wet, and over over £100 dry, per ton, it cost nothing on Islay provided you collected it from the distillery.

and why did they not designate the whole island as an ESA right at the beginning? I do not know, but it was a colossal bureaucratic blunder. What they did was to designate six farms as SSIs and emphasised that there was to be no disturbance of the geese. The farmer would be compensated and all would be well. A firm of land agents was appointed to calculate the losses, and that was that. However, the sum they came up with was derisory and I was asked by the local National Farmers Union to mediate. This I did and produced a figure that was not only accurate but approved by the farmers. It was about five times higher than the original figure and index-linked. It was paid after a long fight, but only after the NCC had burned all its bridges of goodwill, fighting to stop the removal of peat by a distillery. It was felt that by paying up all would be forgiven. I was not very popular with the NCC for a while, but they did ask me to do some work for them at a later date, which I did.

If you allow geese to graze a farm bare and pay the farmer to do so, where do they go for their next meal? Obviously the next farm, which receives no compensation so discontentment becomes the talking point. Various geese-scaring schemes were introduced. People were paid to scare off the geese and now they are counted on each farm monthly and every farmer receives £9 per goose, which costs £290,000 per annum.

My everlasting memories of Islay will always be centred on the kindness and generosity of the Laird, Lord Margadale, and his family, the Morrison family. The woodcock shooting in January is the best in the United Kingdom and I was one of the privileged few people to be asked in January every year. It coincided with the Islay, Jura and Colonsay Agricultural Society Dinner and Annual General Meeting. What fun these were and how we enjoyed them. I spoke once and was amazed to see a bottle of Islay Mist whisky, which had been specially blended for the Laird's 21st birthday, in front of each of us on the table. Fortunately the water was the same colour as the whisky, so it was possible to remain sober.

There were just over 400 spring-calving suckler cows. We made silage and grew enough barley to feed all the cattle, especially the calves, until the following spring. The calves were wintered in a maastock house* for 400 and the cows in special sacrifice areas with concrete floors and feed barriers. Good bulls were used and buyers came from far and wide to the spring sale. The whole farm was run by John MacGillivary, a charming man, and two other excellent young men. These were really fun days and I am so grateful to have been part of such a happy family community.

When the Margadale family were not on Islay I stayed in the Bridgend Hotel, two or three miles from Bowmore. The licensee was the Factor, and

---

* A wooden and slatted prefabricated building for stock, very common in the 1950s and '60s. They were manufactured in Northern Ireland, and sold all over the world.

there was a very good manageress. The food was always good and the company very congenial - a very pleasant place to be.

The great appeal of Islay is its birdlife, truly a delight to any birdwatcher and an added bonus for me when I was there on my trips. The hotel had a special ornithologist's book, and the parties of birdwatchers staying at the hotel, who came from all over the country, twittered and enthused as they made their daily entries in this book! It obviously gave them a great deal of pleasure, while providing amusing reading for the other guests.

I was there on my own one evening when I came across one such entry written by a noble Lord. He had written that while travelling between Bowmore and Bridgend, a distance of some 3 miles, he had seen one barnacle goose (that was not uncommon - there could have been another 20,000 in the area), a Brent goose, which was rare, and a squashed ginger tom. This amused my rather stupid sense of humour, and I was to recall it on a later occasion when making a trip to a hill called Staoisha to see a good herd of Cross Highland heifers.

These cattle were as wild as hell and in order to see them you had to go there early in the morning when they came down to water at the side of the loch. The farm manager picked me up and we went to Port Askaig. On the way I saw a very strange bird, obviously of the starling family, for I had seen many varieties in South Africa. As I did not have my Bannerman books with me, I was lost. When the Factor came along at breakfast time, he was able to tell me that there was a bird expert on the island. He contacted him, and he went along and saw it too. He identified it as a Rosy Pastor starling, the first one ever to be seen on Islay. It just goes to show that if you are up and about early, you may not necessarily catch the worm, but you may catch a rare bird.

The sighting was made more exceptional by the fact that Turkey is the home of this starling, and one not expected to be found on Islay. It was with the common starlings, but the only one of its kind - immensely interesting and exciting. The Factor then wrote in the bird book that on such and such a day, while looking for a squashed ginger tom, Peter Maclaren did, in fact, discover a Rosy Pastor starling.

Some years after I started going to Islay there was a market place built, down on the shore just below Islay House. This was very convenient for Islay Estates because the cattle could be walked along instead of having to go in floats. When the first of the big sales was held, in early May, we were selling stores that had been born the previous spring - about 400 in all.

We chose our auctioneers on the island. Prior to the date of the sale they came round and looked at the stock. As well as the estate cattle, stock from the other farms was sold, and the auctioneers were determined to attract all the buyers they possibly could. Normally the buyers arrived by ferry the previous day, so as an inducement two aeroplanes were chartered.

These aeroplanes, two twin-engined Pipers holding seven people each, took off early on the morning of the sale from Glasgow airport, and one was piloted by an Australian, whom I sat beside.

He flew down over Ayrshire then towards the coast. He kept looking at his maps, so I very boldly said I knew the way, and he promptly replied, 'Well you can damn well fly the thing.' I had never flown a plane before and said so, but he assured me that it was only a case of pushing the joy stick down to go down and pulling it back to go up, pressing your right foot down to make the plane go to the right, and pressing your left foot down to make it go to the left. After that, all I was required to do was to keep an eye on the altimeter, and he would keep a guiding eye on me.

It was a most wonderful day - clear as crystal - one of those early clear May days. I was thoroughly enjoying my little flight, and if the others were aware of what was going on, no one seemed to be jumping up and down the inside. Everyone seemed perfectly happy.

We were flying across the Mull of Kintyre and I asked the pilot if I could take the plane down a bit to see a place I looked after in that area. He said 'Sure', so I turned left and flew down the Mull for a bit. I looked at the forestry and I looked at the low ground farming, all from about 1,000 feet, which was as low as I was allowed or wanted to go. All was very satisfactory, so we flew over Gigha and on to Islay. Because of one hill that is in the way of the airfield if the wind happened to be in the west, I was instructed to 'take her up to 2,000 feet'. I did this and we got over the hill without any problem. Then I was told, 'Take her down to 1,000 feet.' At this point I said that I was most definitely not taking her beyond this and that he would have to take her down and land her himself. He did, of course, take over and we had a very smooth landing.

Islay airport is quite big and was a Costal Command post during the war. We taxied to the end of the runway, then I was asked if I would like to taxi the plane to the Control Tower, which was quite a distance away. 'How the hell do I do that?' I wanted to know. Again I was instructed, 'Set the knob to "Go" and guide it with your feet.'

Well, I must say I did not appreciate how difficult it was to keep a straight course even going at the moderate speed I was travelling at - I was weaving all over the runway. When we eventually got to the other end and to the Control Tower, the chap there looked at me very closely. I felt as if he had come out to smell my breath - he must have thought I had been on the bottle for days.

From the airport we went by car to Bridgend. It was a good sale, which made many people happy, and there was a lot of whisky being liberally dispensed, which suited me well because I was not flying the plane back.

In a merry mood we took our leave around 5.00 pm and flew back to Glasgow. On the way my Australian friend said that he was going to fly alongside the other plane and he would like me to take a photograph of it out of the window. I opened the window and did as I was told, although he did tell me that it was quite against regulations, but I was not daunted. I was never able to find out if it had worked, but I certainly never heard that he had been cashiered or anything. This was only one of many strange and exciting things that happened at the time.

A more unbelievable thing happened when I met up with some Lincolnshire farmers on another trip to the island. I have already mentioned that the Bridgend Hotel was a great place. Lots of parties from the South used to come and take three or four days shooting on the various estates. It was there that they stayed, and where I made the acquaintance of a party from Lincolnshire. They were there to shoot duck at the other end of the island, and they were going out for the morning flight. They had arrived at the hotel before me and it was obvious that they were also set on having a good time, for they had sampled just about every bottle in the place.

Before retiring for the night, the chap who appeared to be the spokesman went round them all and said he would waken them in the morning with a duck decoy 'quack' thing. They were all quite happy about that, but I very politely told him that I certainly wanted no 'quack quacking' at my door. In the morning, sure enough, there was this bloody 'quack quacking' at every door, and my door too, then off they went after breakfast.

I had worked all day and I was relaxing back in the hotel when they came in at the end of a great day's shooting, now hell bent on enjoying themselves. They got absolutely plastered. Half-way through the evening the boss of the group said to me, 'I hear you are going away tomorrow, Peter. Would you like to take my plane up for a flight?' I replied, 'No, not really', but he put his hand in his pocket and produced a large bunch of keys, which looked like car keys, and again repeated the offer. All this time he was weaving about with a decanter of port in one hand and a cigar in the other, not really making a great deal of sense. After a bit of chit-chat, I said, 'You could not possibly fly in your present state'. 'Oh yes,' he said, 'it's only eight hours from bottle to throttle.' This really tickled me and I have never forgotten it. I have often wondered if it was an RAF expression.

I discovered afterwards that this man had truly been a farmer. He had sold land at the top of the market, around 1984/6, and had bought this aeroplane, and used to fly Tony Jacklin, the golfer, all over the place. He was a very good pilot, but I would not like to have seen him in the skies that night.

A year or possibly two later, I was down in Lincolnshire when quite by coincidence I met one of the shooters, who farmed near Grantham, in a pub on the edge of the Fens where I was having a meal. I enquired as to how they had fared on their return journey because I knew that they had planned to fly around Islay on the Sunday, but it was very misty and foggy, so I did wonder about them at the time.

'Oh,' he said, 'we had quite an eventful journey. We had to re-fuel at Glasgow, and at the end of the journey had to crash land, but the dogs, the guns and ourselves were all right. The aeroplane on the other hand was very nearly a write-off!'

It was interesting to meet this chap and hear the end of what had been a very entertaining interlude.

12.
FOLKINGHAM
Crops, concrete and calves

In 1975, when farming looked to be a useful investment, a number of companies thought that they should buy land and farm it. The pension funds were the strongest buyers, followed by insurance companies. Not all made a mess of it, but some did, and after a comparatively short time their land was back on the market.

I was lucky and was asked by a good company that had commissioned a feasibility study that favoured cereals to find a 1,000-acre farm, preferably in Lincolnshire, as the Chairman's relations came from that area. He and I spent about a year looking at farms from the Scottish Borders to Hampshire, but there was always some snag. At the start the agents were never sure whether it was just a valuation job for the bank or a real desire to sell.

There was one farm in Lincolnshire that was in a very run-down state and had been looked at by the agent and the Chairman. The Chairman turned it down flat. I could not be there, but when I was told about it I became very interested. I looked at it with local experts (ICI personnel) and decided that it was a wonderful challenge and could be bought for a not too ridiculous price. It went up for auction and was knocked down very reasonably. My client was to get entry on 2 February 1977.

What attracted me about the farm was that it had been an airfield during the war. It had three rocket sites on it, but above all it had marvellous concrete roads, which were essential if we were to turn it into a good cereal-growing farm, as the land was particularly heavy clay, Grade 2, which was impossible to walk on if it was wet. Little drainage had been done and profits were obviously of no interest as it had been used as a sporting estate with good wild pheasants and both grey and French partridges. The thought of 'hands-on' farming again was very exciting for me, as not only had I been out of touch with real clay for several years, but the challenge was great.

The tractors and implements had to be big and powerful, grain-dryers were established by converting cattle yards, and all the paraphernalia of a modern farm purchased. I wrote to six firms and asked for quotes for all the required machinery, naming types of ploughs, drills, etc, telling them quite bluntly that there were not many orders for £100,000 going about, that they had better sharpen their pencils and that the after service would have to be of the highest order. Only two replied - the others simply did not bother. Strangely enough I had the same thing to do on a large Warwickshire farm two years later, but that time I went round the agents who understood, or if not I made it clear that I wanted their estimates in a hurry. Once again only two agents replied - one actually had the estimate on my desk before I got home. He got the order.

From the time we started we were in a hurry. We had to discard some labour, which is always difficult. We ended up with a manager who became ill and retired within a month, and five able- bodied men. The foreman was an excellent fellow and kept in touch by telephone every day for some weeks. Almost nothing had been sown and we were left with trying to sow spring barley on totally unsuitable land. However, we did it, and it grew when we drained it through the crop and we hoped for the best. We eventually drained the whole farm and grew winter barley, oilseed rape and wheat; the first year's OSR was out of grass fields as we did not intend to have any stock.

We burned all the straw and had to hurry to get everything drilled up before it got too wet in the autumn. We managed it. The biggest problem was the fields, which were very small; we removed hedges and tried to rationalise them to about 40 acres. Some had been less then 5 acres, so it was quite an undertaking. Previously there had been some sugar beet grown, but that was purely for shooting and should never have been grown on the farm as it was impossible to harvest without making a hell of a mess.

Another big problem was weeds, as wild oats and black grass had ruled supreme for years; we had to do a lot of aerial spraying in order to get the crops clean. I became very friendly with the pilot of the aeroplane and for a bottle of whisky he would fly me over the farm every summer so that I could see the wet areas in the fields. It was fascinating.

We purchased the next-door farm and two other areas, one of which was about 6 miles away. We sold it after improvements a few years on, for a good price.

The testing year was 1987, which was an exact repeat scenario of the Scottish harvest of 1985. We were due to lose a lot of money if we could not get the harvest in and were therefore unable to sow the crops for the following year. It was a desperate situation until I asked my pilot friend to put 1 cwt of wheat in the plane and fly over my jacket, which covered about 1 square metre, then count the grains on the jacket. There were 78 in total, so we doubled the amount to equal about 2 cwt per acre. We then broadcast it by plane and harrowed it with a converted all-terrain Land Rover with wide tyres. We therefore managed to sow all the wheat, which was a miracle, and, what is more, it yielded well.

The airfield covered about 300 acres and had been sown to grass after it had been constructed, but what the devil were we going to do with all the concrete runways and dispersal points round the perimeter? The fall was 16 feet from north to south and concrete would obviously cost a lot of money to reclaim. I asked the Board and they said, 'Take it up and dump it.' Fortunately I heard in a pub one night that contractors were looking for concrete to use on the Grantham bypass, so I told them about ours and they paid us £300 an acre to bomb it, crush it and cart it away. It is marvellous what you can pick up in the local! It was cleared very well, and any unwanted limestone was tipped on the rocket sites, sort of land-scaped and planted with trees and shrubs as nesting cover and for ameni-ty purposes. There was no way we could break up 16 feet of reinforced concrete ourselves.

We also had other distractions all over the farm: machine-gun posi-tions, odd maintenance buildings and the WAAF site. I could never understand why the WAAFs required so many loos, but some wise person explained that when reveille was sounded in the morning there had to be sufficient for a lot of desperate ladies. They were also built of reinforced concrete, so could not be broken up very easily. We dug trenches 14 feet deep, bulldozed the concrete in, scraped soil over the top and returned the area to the field. It was a very exciting time and when we had finished we had transformed a bleak, barren area into a good well-roaded farm, pro-ducing good yields. I was told that one particular field would grow noth-ing, but its first wheat crop exceeded 4 tons per acre.

There was a good stock of wild pheasant on the farm and by supple-menting the woods with strips of kale we could have some good shooting. In a good year we could have two days, in bad years only one. We shot cocks and hens and the bags were good. We actually shot 200 twice, and an average of 100-120 over all the years. They flew well and, as it was usu-ally blowing a gale, they were the greatest fun. Six guns were all that were required, which was a welcome change from most syndicates' shoots, which never seemed to shoot with less than eight or nine.

After a few years, when we had sold the outlying farm of 280 acres for a good price, we reinvested the money by building a slatted-floor bull and fattening building that had pens for 600 bulls, a huge slurry lagoon and two silos for 2,000 tons. We started with the Rosemaund system of fat-tening Friesian bull calves that had been purchased on contract at about ten weeks old, brought on in bedded loose-boxes, then put on to the slats at about 20 weeks old. We fed all the cheap food from citrus fruit to

McCain's chips, potato mash and peas - you name it and we fed it - and we only had a complaint once when we were told that the bulls tasted of marmalade! We had, of course, been feeding them oranges.

It became obvious that we would have to put a grassland break into the system, in the first place to put three-year leys for silage, and in the second place to put permanent grass back on the airfield. The reason for this sudden apparent change was that we found it extra difficult to buy the right sort of calves for the beef unit. To have a suckler herd of our own seemed to make sense, so we purchased 100 Hereford/Friesian heifers and three bulls, two Charolais and one Romanogla for comparison.

The cows had to be out-wintered, so with the advice of Dr Mike Kelly from the West of Scotland Agricultural College, who came with me to look at the site, we erected the cheapest form of suckler housing that I had ever seen. We found a concrete area and we bulldozed soil to 10 or 12 feet round it. Within that area we put up four yards capable of holding 25 suckler cows. There were feeding passages down the middle and on either side, and shelter was provided by two half-ton Hestan bales on the sides, and the pens defined with second-hand crash-barrier rails off the motorway. It worked perfectly, and should be a lesson to others who spend a hell of a lot of money on fancy buildings in areas of low rainfall. The cattle were paddock-grazed in good-sized blocks, with mains-powered electric fences. This system was a winner.

We were asked by the Anglian Water Board if they could build a sewage tank, really a reservoir and quite a big one, behind one of the rocket sites so that it could not be seen, and was not, therefore, environmentally unfriendly. It was all wired round with safety netting, etc, and was filled twice a year. There was no smell, and we got a lot of free fertiliser, of course, which improved the farm so much that we built our own as well and both tanks kept most of the arable and grass land fertilised. If sprayed on the surface the smell was appalling, so it was injected into the soil and, providing that there were enough tankers to ply back and forth, the operation went very smoothly. This was a very good and cheap way to fertilise a farm. I am confident that more of this will have to be done in the future as no longer will the Anglian Water Board or any other water board be allowed to tip sewage into the sea.

The story of the Lincoln farm would not be complete without telling the story of all the drama after the Board of Directors had given permission to clear the airfield. To my mind the clearing of the airfield for cropping was an absolute priority, and the sooner we got started the better. The farm manager at the time was told to get on with it and to hire the necessary machinery.

I was in the habit of going down once a month, and on this particular occasion I was meeting with the draining officer from ADAS. When I arrived I was livid to discover that there was only one bloody digger to clear 300 acres with concrete perimeter track and dispersal points and to level it all out. I told the draining officer, and he too was hopping mad. We rushed into the farm office, seized the Yellow Pages and telephoned round the people we could find within a 100-mile radius, looking for those who could provide us with the best type of machinery. Eventually we found a firm in Northampton, run by a Scotsman called McKenzie, which was fortunate.

We told them what we wanted - two earth-movers, the type seen working on motorways, two bulldozers and all the other ancillary equipment - and that we wanted it immediately. Could he do it? Yes. His men started the next day. All the equipment arrived, plus caravans for the men - quite a conglomeration. They started every morning at 5.00 am and by the end of the first week the difference was incredible.

The cost of such an operation was high - an agreement of £22 per hour had been reached for the operating machinery. This was fine until it rained; when I telephoned the farm manager to enquire how things were going, I heard that not a wheel had turned for three or four days, and that it would now cost us a heck of a lot more. Why? Apparently the same charge applied even if they were only standing around waiting for the rain to cease. This was totally unacceptable, so I telephoned their head office and had a word with Mr MacKenzie. I enquired as to the possibility of his machines going elsewhere until the weather conditions were right. This did not suit him, so after some skilful negotiations, a bargain of £11 per hour while at a standstill was agreed! After that everything went smoothly until the job was completed.

I had another client who farmed in the East Midlands. It was a large farm with 2,000 acres of cereals, 300 acres of sugar beet and over 300 acres of irrigated potatoes, as well as a dairy and a large sheep enterprise of 1,500 grey-faced ewes. It had not been farmed well and the agent asked me to have a look, do a feasibility study and forecast what profits they could make. This I did, and he and the owner liked what they saw and asked me to find a farm manager who would be capable enough to carry out the plan and acceptable to everyone concerned. This was duly carried out.

On one of my visits I suggested that I should drive the owner round the estate and show her what had been done. The lady had no interest in the actual farm, but she was very keen that everything on the estate should be well looked after: woods, forestry on the poorer land, the shooting, cottages and buildings in general. Before we set off she told me the following story.

One afternoon when she was driving round the estate she came upon half-ton potato boxes smashed, with the contents scattered far and wide, so she went on and eventually passed a tractor and trailer, going like a bat out of hell, shedding boxes at an alarming rate. After managing to pass and stop the tractor, she told the driver what was happening. His reply was 'Ah, shit', which left my friend speechless.

On the day we went round we inspected the new dairy - it was a one-man/150-cow affair. We looked at the beef fattening cattle, bulls from the dairy herd and some Charolais cross cattle, the sheep and then the crops. All went well until we passed the potato store, which looked as if RAF Harriers had been practising bombing prior to the Falklands War. I apologised for the mess and explained that we were changing from half-ton to one-ton boxes. At that moment she shouted, 'There he is - "Ah, shit"!' I had a few nervous moments before I realised that it was the tractor driver to whom she was referring, and all I could do was express my surprise that he was still on the payroll. We did have a laugh about it afterwards, and the story has been repeated many a time since.

13.
FUN, SHOOTING AND DOGS
The agony and the ecstasy

One of the most entertaining tasks I had as a consultant was running a shoot. I loved it. For a few years I ran a shoot in Fife for a client who did not live there. It was marvellous ground, mostly hard woods on very steep ground, so the pheasants were exceptionally good. We let it for all but two days, which the owner kept for himself; he always asked me to shoot, which was very kind of him. The whole experience gave me an insight into how to achieve the very best out of a shoot by managing it properly.

The late Colonel Bill Stirling of Keir was always looking for really good shoots to entertain his unrivalled teams of European and American guns. He took the Fife shoot, supplied the loaders and the transport, and we supplied the beaters and the eight pickers-up, because we never ran through the woods the following day. We had to see what the guns could do and had two beats and shot them separately unless there was some reason to have the very best guns on a certain day. The bags were never excessive, starting with 250 to 300 from approximately 4,000 reared, rising to nearly 6,000.

One very special day we had an important French party, which included their Government's Finance Minister. Bill asked me to look after her, so I placed her at her peg for the first drive and started to chat her up. I asked her why she had come to Scotland to shoot our pheasants, and her immediate reply was, 'Your pheasants are so marvellous.' As it was the time of the first 'lamb war' I ventured to ask her why France was being so difficult. I knew it was a risky question. She wagged her finger at me as if I was a naughty boy and said, 'That is a completely different subject.'

On the last day of the season in 1980, Bill, his brother, a French Count, another chap, my son and I, shooting the best ground for the third day that week, shot 264 pheasants, mostly cocks. It was an exhilarating day and one I shall always remember. Running the shoot entailed driving through Edinburgh over the bridge and along a poor road of 117 miles, morning and evening. We always had a splendid lunch, with wine and port to fortify us. It was all great fun and good for my Labradors. Latterly Bill and I would stand behind the guns and shoot some impossibly high birds, but that was only on special occasions.

On many a long winter's evening Jean is truly amazed as she hears me chuckling as I look through my game books, which I started to keep in 1935. I do not mention how I shot, but often how we all shot, then I recall the fun we had and why they were such memorable days.

While doing this I remember also all the dogs I have had, and what immeasurable pleasure they have given me, and these ramblings would not be complete without them. I have never been without at least one dog; once we had five, two Labradors and three Jack Russell terriers, two of which, Midge and Twiggy, were great characters.

Midge had three puppies, but we kept only one. At that time a bachelor friend asked if we would look after a German boy who was about the same age as our younger ones. We agreed and had him for about two weeks. He was a difficult boy; he would not help with any of the household chores, saying they was 'Vimin's Vork', so our boys were not amused. The puppy was called Twiggy, but I always called her 'Wee One'. She used to sit on my knee, and was always given odd titbits whenever she was about. The German boy heard me repeatedly saying or calling 'Wee One', but it was on the day he left when Jean and a friend were taking him to the station at Dumfries that he asked as they went down the drive why Mr Maclaren kept saying 'We won'. Fortunately Jean and her friend realised what he thought I had been saying, and that the silly boy had thought I was referring to the war!

All shooting men should have a dog, especially the rough shooters who do not wish to leave anything they may have wounded. Pheasant shooting, of course, is different, as there are always pickers-up behind the guns.

I had golden retrievers and spaniels, all as wild as hell, before we moved to Cheshire, where I bought a good Labrador bitch and bred from her; two of her puppies went to America. From then on I was smitten by them. I bred some, but was very generously given others. One was a golden Labrador called Flapper. She arrived in a box and in a terrible condition, thin and emaciated, and when we fed her she came up in lumps. She was gun-shy, but with kindness and perseverance, she turned out to be a wonderful water dog and marvellous for duck flighting.

A good friend, who is sadly now dead, had a big black bitch called Sally. She was a good-looking lady but she had one fault, she was a tremendous farter. Now, as I always keep the dogs in the house we wondered whether or not we could bear it, but bear it we did.

One day I was on a shoot with Barbara Harcourt-Wood, the very well-known Labrador breeder. She was picking up on that day and we got talking. She saw poor old Sally, who should by then have been pensioned off, and to my amazement and eternal gratitude she offered me a seven-year-old bitch called Glenfarg Ripple. She had won one trial and had then been used exclusively for breeding. The Glenfarg Labradors were famous - the combination of Barbara's ability to pick and breed only the best, coupled with Meldrum's expert training, made the dogs famous all over the world. I was thrilled when I was given Ripple; I realised that she was something very special and that I must try and treat her and handle her as well as Barbara had done. Fortunately I had her during the good grouse years, as it is on the moor that one can really see a dog work at its best.

I remember three of the most extraordinary retrieves I had ever seen, and another one at North Sanquhar which I was reminded of by a keeper not long ago.

The first was at Braco when I was shooting with Robin Muir. Robin and I were great friends and we shot everywhere together - our wives rarely saw us during the season. This occasion was on the second drive known as 'The Flat'. I was on the left and another very keen dog man, Admiral Sir David Gregory, in the butt on my right. Someone shot a snipe that fell somewhere over a fence and burn and into a patch of rushes. Could either of us get it? It was fully half a mile away and the direction was sketchy to say the least, so I said I would try from where I was standing. The Admiral laughed and said 'Not a hope'. I told Ripple to 'get out' so off she went, flat out; when she was a long way out, I stopped her with one blast of a whistle. She looked round and with arm directions I sent her on. She crossed a wire fence and a burn and I stopped her in the area of rushes where I had been told that the snipe had fallen. She hunted it thoroughly, then moved on, put her head down and came racing back with the bird. David Gregory was very generous with his praise and we often talked about it later.

The other episode was on the second day of our four-day shoot on Donside. It was after the first drive, which had been a good one, and there were quite a number of birds to pick round the butt area. My loader had a very good spaniel, so he picked the close-in birds and I sent Ripple for one that was a fair way out in some peat haggs*. She searched for ages but failed to find it; it could not have been dead and had obviously gone to ground in a hole in the haggs. Unfortunately the head keeper, who also had Glenfarg dogs, had seen all this happening, and when we were on the way down he said, 'I thought that was a good bitch you had.' I insisted that she was, but he was not impressed.

As luck would have it, at the next drive he was flanking on the right and I was in the right-hand butt. He flagged a pair up towards me; they

* Boggy areas from which peat has been dug.

were wide but I managed to kill both, although untidily. The first towered and fell behind the butt, and the second carried on down, crossed a burn and fell in some heather. I never moved until he came up and asked if I was going to pick them up.

I said, 'Of course, but from the butt.'

He laughed and said, 'I want to see this.'

I climbed on to the butt and sent Ripple off for the towered one. Distances are always difficult to judge, but I got it about right and she picked it up at once and returned with it. I then sent her off again for the second bird, which was more difficult, but in moments she had picked it up and was back, leaving the head keeper flabbergasted. My loader and I were bursting with pride.

I had Ripple for only three seasons from 1965 to 1968. She died of a massive internal haemorrhage when jumping a stone dyke as we went round the farm. I cried like a child.

Barbara at once came to my rescue and gave me Ripple's daughter, Ruffle. She was good, but not as good as her mother. I have always had, and still have, good dogs, home-bred, keeper-trained and self-trained, but none have equalled Ripple's intelligence.

I have a good dog just now, bought after my previous one died. She was supposed to be gun-shy and as wild as a hawk, but would make an excellent companion-friend.

One day I was having lunch with my daughter and her husband at their home on a shooting day, and as the first drive after lunch was just outside the house, I took my Labrador Bea along and stood behind to watch. There was a picker-up there with four Labradors who seemed to be doing a good job, but Bea was watching and when he had finished I sent her out for what she had seen. She immediately came back with a dead hen pheasant, then went off on her own to pick up what she thought was a wounded bird. She was right, the bird was wounded and she had brought it back. We look forward to more happy days picking up.

The years 1957, 1975, 1960 and 1963 were excellent grouse years. In 1957 I went off to the Borders one day. It was a glorious morning, and I had left The Leaths early. As the day progressed the wind began to rise; we were actually at the tail end of a hurricane called Debbie, which blew at 90 miles an hour. We had all shot fairly well, even under those conditions, but one of the guns was determined to find out from the experts at Farnborough how fast those grouse were actually flying, so he wrote to them and the reply appeared in *The Field*. They said they did 50 miles per hour on the flat, and taking the gale rate into account that would be 140 miles per hour. If, however, they were going down hill, depending on the angle, a third more could be added on, so these grouse were, in fact, doing very nearly 200 miles per hour, and yet we were shooting them. You could only shoot them with the wind; it was quite impossible, of course, to shoot against the wind. Wonderful years!

Another marvellous character lived near Dumfries. He had been a prisoner of the Japanese in the war, but it had not impaired his great sense of humour - he was always ready to do anything for a laugh. At the end of one season five guns were shooting cock pheasants only, and we shot more than 100. We also shot a sparrowhawk, which nowadays we would have been condemned for, and probably hung, drawn and quartered. In addition I shot a fox in one of the drives, as there was no hunting anywhere near there.

Anyway, we had some refreshments before we said our thanks and I went off in my Dormobile. It appeared not to be going very well so I stopped at the end of the drive to look at the engine; I thought that perhaps one of the plug leads had come off. Instead, when I put my hand inside I found the fox tied right across the engine - it was beginning to pong a bit too. I simply burst out laughing, then I thought, 'I'll fix him.' I went back to the house, but wise man that he was, he had locked all the doors, so I could not put the thing in the loo, the idea being that in the morning he would find the head staring up at him from the pan.

In 1959 some of the good shots in Scotland had been asked by ICI to go to a shoot at Damerham, south of Salisbury; that was in the early days of the game conservancy, and it was an ICI shoot. It was a wonderful still day with the partridges flying beautifully. We did not do ourselves or our reputations any harm, but it was a great experience to see how a big and professional partridge shoot was run. They were all wild partridges, which is very different from what happens nowadays.

After the Damerham partridge shoot we were taken to Salisbury station with our guns, bags, etc, and still wearing our shooting clothes. There were only three guns from Scotland and as the General Election was the next day we all had to rush back home to do our various duties.

The three of us were not small, one was 6 foot 6 inches, the other 6 foot 3 inches and myself a mere 6 foot 2 inches. We managed to get a 1st Class compartment to ourselves, and after a few refreshments we decided that we must change into our London suits as we were going to have dinner at one of the smart London clubs. We duly pulled down the curtains, took off our shooting clothes and emerged as eye-catching as butterflies from rather ugly chrysalises. After an excellent dinner we joined our various night sleepers for home. Quite a day.

On another occasion I was invited by a friend to shoot grouse on Donside where they had shot a lot of grouse earlier. He picked a team of guns and we set off and had four tremendous days. The weather was good, frosty in the mornings with no mist, but on the last day it blew an absolute gale. Unknown to us the very efficient loaders had been keeping account of the birds we had shot and the number of cartridges we had fired, so on the last morning, when the wind had got up and rather spoiled things, we were told that they had a lot of money on us. I was behind by two or some such number.

My chap said, 'You bloody well have to shoot really well. I want to win all the money.'

When we stopped at lunchtime it was still anybody's game, but we were told that in the afternoon we were going to see an enormous number of grouse, so we took 300 cartridges up for two drives. I remember very well that I had a rotten butt. I was on the top side and I thought, 'Good Lord, I will not get many here.'

I offered my friend a fiver for his butt, but he could not be persuaded. He said, 'Not on your life!' He wanted to win. I shot a few grouse and he shot a few, but by then they were coming down wind and rather across.

At the next drive my loader either confused the head keeper about butt numbers or bribed him to give me the best in the line. It was a large circular stone butt and could hold three people with ease. The wind was gale force and wrong for the drive as it took most of the birds out to the right, making them impossible to flank as they would be too high. The head keeper, the one who had seen my dog work so well, came and sat in the butt to watch the drive. The first lot, a small pack, came high, wide and handsome, and by some miracle I managed to get four with my two guns. Many more came and I had a wonderful drive. My loader had won the jackpot and I topped it with an extra-large tip. It was a great ending to a wonderful day.

Another friend and I had a shoot in Gatehouse of Fleet for several years. It had not really been looked after in years, but we took it on and reared a few pheasants in the old-fashioned way. The owner of the land had a keeper, and between them they looked after the vermin. We also had our own keeper, a local man who got on well with everybody.

Those few years were good, not due to enormous bags but because the owner was an amiable character, by profession a law graduate from Edinburgh. He had been at St Valerie at the start of the war, was captured and remained a prisoner-of-war right through to the end. He decided at that time that on his return home he would farm, as his family already had an estate. This he did and jolly well too. We took the shooting on his land, but if he or his boys were at home, they joined us.

He was a wonderful man, madly keen on the outdoors. He always wore a moleskin waistcoat, made from moles caught on his own land. He never wore a cap, but sported a plastic bag on his head.

The strange thing about this chap was that he always had some animal in tow. He became enamoured with wild goats, and ended up with a little kid, which was virtually his shadow. It was a mutual admiration, and to take his little kid in a van or car was a great delight. When it did go in a vehicle, however, it generally misbehaved, and fired off some 'bullets'. If and when it did, we had to stop instantly and count. If the number went over the previous total, then that was a new record and there would be cheering and clapping. Glorious days and tremendous fun!

14.
BROOKLANDS, THE BRAE
AND RETIREMENT

Open gardens, kind hearts and lazy days

Brooklands was a truly lovely place, a light, airy 19th-century house with marvellous views and lovely amenity grounds. When we bought it we promised to retain the gardener, Ernest Binks, for the two years until he retired. We hoped that he would look after the garden in the same immaculate way that he had for over 20 years.

The amazing story of Ernest Binks's gardening years started when he was employed by Brigadier and Mrs Jebb at The Birks in Northumberland as a gamekeeper. He also used to ride as second horseman when Mrs Jebb was hunting. He was a good cricketer and a marvellous countryman of the old school. Above all, he had green fingers, so when Mrs Jebb decided to leave Northumberland and to buy Brooklands, he was asked to come with them as gardener. He took to his new job with great enthusiasm, and was still there when Mrs Jebb died, so we were more than happy to take him on, as we knew very little about gardening. It was wonderful for us that he never retired, and we worked, learned and watched what he did for 11 happy years! He was such a great man. When I said that it was a pity that only half the walled garden was being used, he immediately said, 'We must plant it up with good things.' This we did and went on and on, always with his approval and co-operation.

The first time I met Binks I liked him and he liked us as a family, which was exactly what Mrs Jebb had wanted. We were encouraged by him to renovate the pond at the lodge and stock it with trout, plant trees, enlarge the woods and really try to look after the place as it deserved. What fun it all was and yet, when things went wrong, as they did sometimes, such as big trees blowing over and smashing some precious plants, Binks was never downhearted. He would clear up the mess and persuade us that it would be for the best in the end. What is more, he was right.

His passion was fishing, and he warned us that if we ever saw all the garden tools lying around without him, he would be away with his friend who lived in the village, because the River Urr was just right and full of fish. He rarely came back in those days without a fish, and we of course benefited. The tools were always back in the shed by night time.

We doubled the garden in size, and planted more good large-leaved rhododendrons and other trees until we had 1½ acres of walled garden and an additional 6 acres of kept borders full of rich and rare plants, as well as a large area of grass to cut.

It was a wonderful way to relax at weekends and whenever I was at home. For the last five years, when it was gradually becoming too much for us, once more we were fortunate to have a wonderful young gardener - a young man called Steve Harrison. Steve not only did more and more as I did less and less, but also produced 3,000 plants for sale and for our own replacements. Goodness knows how he did it - his own garden at the lodge was always full of plants and always tidy. It was the greatest fun working with him and I miss him, and he misses us, I believe.

Jean, who has been, and still is, a long-suffering wife, is artistic and was obviously as keen as me to have the garden looking well. Without her we should have been lost, as her artistic eye kept the planting of all things just right. We never planted without first seeking approval from the 'planning officer', as we called her.

Through our gardening interest we met and made friends with many charming people from all over the world, and visited many good gardens around the country. Brooklands was a very happy place and we enjoyed every minute of our time there, even when it snowed or blew gales and wrought destruction, which it frequently did as the 500-foot contour ran through the garden. *Country Life* included an article on the gardens, so we must have got it reasonably right!

We opened our garden to the public every year for Scotland's Garden Scheme; we sold plants and made a great deal of money for charities. Over 1,000 people turned up in 1993, our last opening to the public, and we made £3,770.

The following article was written for the Red Cross in 1990. It sums up all the work that had to be done before and during every Open Day. Thank goodness it was only one day a year.

Very foolishly I agreed to write a short article for your excellent newspaper, on what actually happens both before and on the day. I might have included the post-opening feeling of 'Thank heavens that is over. Never again. Why do we do it?'

The whole operation actually starts a year before when we begin to prepare for the plant sales, which are really the backbone of the financial success of the day. A good day brings people who wish to have a day out, meet their friends and look at the general effect of the place. A fair or even wet day still brings masses of people if they know that there are good plants to buy or to see in the garden. A really sizzling hot day has the same effect on numbers as a poor day, because Mum and Dad have to take the children to the sea. So one hopes for a fair day, preferably with sun so that people come, sit around and hopefully enjoy the outing.

The organisation for the day is damnable. We have to clear a room for the teas, so the dogs and I are miserable because we like to sit in the window seats either sleeping or writing some report of immense interest to somebody, or so I hope. Chairs and tables are brought in from the village hall, fortunately by a kind neighbour who carries them into the house. No sooner are they in than I am told that there must be chairs for the older people to sit on if by chance we have a good day, so out go some which are strategically placed.

However, before this the house smells like a bakery. Hundreds of biscuits are produced for the invading hordes to demolish with their tea. Plates and cups and all other utensils are laid out as an army of charming and dedicated ladies come and work like slaves, dishing out tea and washing and drying up. God bless them. Without them, we would be lost.

'GARDEN OPEN' signs are erected in strategic places in the morning, tables are put out with cash for the entrance money, plant money, tea money, but the loos are free! The police are alerted and hopefully supply some signs and help with the traffic, because unless people use the one-way system we have the most awful snarl-ups. One must insist on entering by the lodge and going out by the back gate - quite simple if everyone does it.

Two good and trusted friends are given a cash box with the tickets and sit collecting the money as the invaders arrive. They work hard and have to see that no one gets in without paying. There are also replacements standing by to relieve the first two if they get exhausted.

The plants have somehow been moved from the garden to the tennis court. Over 1,000 of them are laid out so that people can see them and, most importantly, what they cost. One plant in every lot is named and buyers are encouraged not to take the name tags but to write one for themselves with the labels supplied. It is absolutely infuriating if the original label is removed or put back where it does not belong. Three people are required to sell the plants and one, most fortunately, collects the 'lolly'. Another kind lady sits at the door taking the tea money and enjoys herself chatting to her friends as they come in. I float about in the garden trying to answer questions and appear, hopefully, very knowledgeable. The latter does not last very long as invariably many people know a lot more about plants than I do, so I learn a lot of things I did not know.

Soon after 5.00 pm, when all are completely exhausted and in need of stronger refreshment than tea, the money is counted. The rivalry between gate, as we call it, and the plant stall is intense as a friendly bank manager and the plant lady add it all up. Excitement rises, more refreshment is required, and the figure is known. 'Hurrah!' we all shout. We have broken our record. What about another glass to celebrate? But alas, all is not finished. Some of us have to take down all the signs that were so carefully put up in the morning, and tomorrow hopefully get the tea room back to normal for me and the dogs.

'Is it all worth it?' you ask. Yes, it is. It gives us an excuse to keep the place tidy and to let people come and enjoy an afternoon out and a garden looking well (or so we hope) and the satisfaction of providing a sizeable cheque for the chosen charity. 'Will you do it next year?' you ask. In the general state of euphoria everyone says 'Yes, of course we must', so we will.'

Robert Urquhart, writing in *The Scotsman* when I retired from ICI, said, 'He is operating from Brooklands, Crocketford, Dumfriesshire, which, in spite of his new busy life, I am sure will be a garden showplace as good as any in Scotland.' His forecast was fully vindicated.

No doubt you are wondering how Jean managed in the house with all these activities going on. Well, not only did we retain the services of the gardener, but also those of a wonderful daily help, Mrs Mary Kerr. Mrs Kerr, or Doc as she was fondly called, had, like Binks, been with Mrs Jebb for over 20 years, and then took us over! We could not have found a more loyal and devoted person. In fact, she was a good friend to the whole family. Nothing ruffled her, and she could always rise to the occasion, and this was a great help to Jean.

Sadly, however, there comes a time when we have to give up the things we enjoy - I believe it is called 'Anno Domini'. So, at the beginning of May 1993, after a lot of work on the glossy brochures, Brooklands was put on the market.

All the photographs had been taken on 18 May 1992, and it took much careful deliberation before finally choosing the right ones. I think we did just that, for the agents were swamped with requests for the brochures, and all 500 went very quickly.

We were wise not to state the asking price in the advertisements as all but three contenders were frightened off. One put on a closing date for 27 May 1993, and this we honoured. Thus Brooklands was sold, but we were still looking around for a suitable house for our retirement, and to date we

had found the ones on the market to be either too big or poky and claus-
trophobic, and there was certainly nowhere locally big enough to take the
furniture and pictures with which we did not wish to part. Then someone
told us about The Brae. It looked huge from the outside, but when we
viewed it we found that inside it would be, with some modifications, just
the right size. We were delighted.

After a lot more work than we had bargained for, we moved in on 27
September. A 30-year guarantee for dry rot, which had been extensive, a
new roof, complete rewiring and re-plumbing and gas central heating
should, we hope, see us protected from house problems for the rest of our
life!

The Brae was built in 1803. It has a field of nearly an acre in front
between the house and the road, and rather more behind the house. The
garden was in pretty poor shape, with the most impoverished soil I had
ever come across, but I know that with time, patience and effort it can be
made good.

Our Labrador, Bea, was not very taken with it at first, as she missed her
half-mile run up the drive from the lodge, and her walks round the garden
and through the rhododendrons. However, to compensate we take her
now in the car to where she can run along forestry roads. This pleases her
and keeps her in good trim.

The removal from Brooklands was something of a nightmare and without the help of the family and Lisa, our one-time nanny who lives locally, we could never have managed. I am thankful to say that Lisa has now
agreed to come back to us in our retirement.

The actual trauma of moving was greater than we expected, and I
ended up back in hospital - the best hospital, as far as I am concerned,
anywhere. When I read or listen to the media condemning the National
Health Service, it makes me absolutely mad. There is never anything con-
structive said, and most of the time is spent running it down. How wrong
they are. The Dumfries & Galloway Royal Infirmary is a first-class hospital. Nothing is too much trouble for them to test, scan or whatever. The
doctors and surgeons rank among the best in the country, and some go all
over the world to examine, train or even operate. A more dedicated group
of people you could not find.

The student nurses receive an excellent training; some stay on while
others go further afield. They are mostly local and a good number of farmers' daughters and wives are amongst them. Country people are always
cheery and kind. I hate hospitals, but would settle for a permanent stay in
either the Intensive Care Unit or Ward Ten if under the command of the
two present Sisters whose knowledge, discipline and good humour could
never be surpassed.

The thought of no more work was alarming. I was ordered to do nothing, but what is nothing? My consultancy with all its travelling had to
cease, and gardening, even with all the available aids, was too strenuous.

However, hope springs eternal, and one day, quite unexpectedly, came a wonderful letter from a client, suggesting that I be retained as their consultant. What a lifeline when I was feeling low! I accepted with gratitude, and can only trust that I will be able to repay his faith in me.

Now, of course, I have more time for the grandchildren who are growing up very fast. It is a great joy to Jean and me to watch them and to have them around. It helps to keep our outlook young!

15.
VIEWPOINT

Pernicious progress

(Written for the *Galloway News* in July 1994)

I really do not know why I was asked to write this piece, in fact I was a silly ass as I had not quite finished the book I had been working on, *Sixty Years of Farming, Fun and Frustration*. Whether it ever gets published and I am allowed to keep my title is another matter.

It starts with farming, or should I say learning to farm, in the Stewartry in 1936. Although over the years I did actually farm in many different places, I came back to within a mile of my 'alma mater' in 1952, having been involved locally from 1947 when I was with ICI.

There have been many changes, some obviously for the good, but there are many on the down side, especially the eroding of the countryside, and by that I do not mean environmentally but by the relentless and quite necessary progress and better ideas, better houses, better working conditions and then, of course, the war, which made agriculture the top priority, and those of us who were involved did have to change our ways. There was the 'grow food at any cost' campaign and, coupled with that, very little labour available to work on farms, so change and mechanism became imperative. They were stirring times. These changes and how I see the future form the basis of this article, coupled with the urbanisation and consequent ruination of the true country way of life caused mainly by ignorant conservationists with ignorant planners who change for political, not practical, reasons.

I would like to highlight the changes I have seen and to remind people of the consequences of those changes; also if possible to describe why they had to be made. Finally, who, at the end of those changes, will survive?

Agriculture in the next century will be very different, but traditional skills, stockmanship, etc, will still have to be there. It is the additional skills to survive that will prove more difficult.

When the SMMB was formed in 1933 it proved to be the salvation of the South West, as previously milk was sold to Glasgow and the North of England or wherever a market could be found. Most of it went by rail in 17-gallon churns, so it was a labour-intensive job.

There were still quite a few farmers making cheese, and others sold their milk to local creameries who eventually were bought by the SMMB who acquired creameries for £200,000 payable with a loan at 3 per cent over 20 years. There were also Cheese Factors who took most of the farm-made Cheddar and guaranteed a market for it. The Board expanded and, when other surplus milk was available, butter and cream were produced at some of the creameries, so the market was completely covered.

From that time onwards the dairy farmers began to prosper, and all farming prospered during the war years. The war and the war effort certainly were beneficial to English farmers. I know, because I was looking after nearly 1,300 acres that had not been well farmed. The ploughing out of grassland, as directed by the WAR AGs, put a tremendous pressure on farms that had a dwindling labour force and had to learn how to handle cereals in a big way. There were only 30 combine harvesters operating in the whole of the United Kingdom at the beginning, but the numbers increased rapidly as and when there was space on ships to import them.

Milking machines came in between the wars and obviously reduced the labour requirements on most dairy farms, but dairying remained a highly labour-intensive enterprise until pipeline milking and bulk tanks became available in the 1950s.

The other major changes were when barley became the common cereal, replacing oats and wet grain stores, and finally traditional hay-making was replaced with the square baler. The growing of swedes carried on well into the 1960s, and were then replaced by silage, which has replaced hay as the main source of forage conservation. I remember only too well the difficulties of early days with ropy and unreliable machinery, no buck-rakes or rotary mowers and unsatisfactory cutting and blowing machines. It was not until the Lundell arrived from America, when we could use direct-cut flail mowers and blowers, that the dramatic changes we now see became commonplace. Silos both open and covered were erected, and only the weather and the effluent disposal became serious problems for the more go-ahead farmers, and still remain so today as forage conservation is of vital importance to most stock farmers.

The down side, unhappily, was the demise of the corncrakes in the district. I remember only too well our last birds at The Leaths, and was heartbroken to see the hen bird and her eggs destroyed in the silage field. Partridges, which were plentiful, fared as badly, and although fields were cut so as to allow nesting birds to be seen and not killed, the eggs were saved and some of us hatched them out and reared them, but mostly to no avail. After release when fully feathered they seem to disappear.

On the stock side there were major changes; loose-housing and cubicles for the dairy cows became the thing for the 1960s, allowing dairymen to look after more stock. This figure has risen from low numbers to up to 150 cows per man at present. Hill shepherds are now herding 1,000 ewes per man and more, provided that there are ATVs and reasonable in-bye paddocks to aid them. Clipping is done with the help of New Zealand clippers, who go from farm to farm and charge on a per-head basis. Where lambing is inside, extra labour is taken on to ensure lambing percentages are much higher than they were in the 1970s and '80s. Even this year, which was the worst in living memory, I know of one flock of 1,089 greyfaces that, with only 23 yeld*, produced 203 per cent at marking.

Beef cattle are being looked after in larger numbers. Fattening systems have changed with the introduction of bigger sheds with drive-through feeder wagons and even outside feeder areas, either built on to existing sheds or outside on concrete pads. It is all change. It had to change. Good men were not too easy to find, and when they were everything had to be done to make their job easier.

When I was asked to write this I was brought two copies of previous articles to show me what was required. I read both with great interest. One was serious and asked some questions, while the other was humorous. I cannot respond to the humorous one as all he asked for was a good day for the Dumfries Show.

The serious one was about the question of joining the Farmers Producer Groups and posed the question of the stock on the writer's farm. The question was, and I quote, 'Whether to run an economic unit on its own or whether to tie up other producers in the same field in order to satisfy the market demand for their products'. I have preached the need for groups and actually set up and ran two big ones, with over 1,000 suckler cows, some 20 years ago. In those days it was easier to get started. A good feasibility cash flow and animal flow were precursors to getting started.

Now, despite extra and quite generous Government grants, they are more difficult to get started. The main difficulties, as I see it, are that farmers still wish to keep their independence, like going to market, and distrust the deadweight system of selling. There is no need for any of those points to be stumbling blocks. They should wish to know the deadweight of the stock they sell. They should take an interest and bother to go and see their stock hanging up, or they can sell live on the electronic markets and see them on the screen. They can still go to the auction market to compare prices, but they must remember that it is time-consuming and prices at market on the day may vary and be up or down on what the group is offering that week. In my view those are difficulties that can be

* Not in lamb.

easily overcome. However, there are others that should be overcome and could be rectified by a common sense approach from some civil servants and the Scottish Office.

I have been one of a team involved in setting up a marketing group lately. It took over 18 months of hard work and pressurising by people other than myself to get it off the ground in 1993. The requirement for a vast number of Board members is plain stupid, as a Board of five with an outside businessman, not necessarily connected to agriculture, is quite enough to dictate policy, see that it is carried out and look after the finances. Why have any more? They are a nuisance and only hinder. I would suggest that interested people get in touch with the local marketing livestock group, and I am sure they can satisfy all their needs.

In earlier years the groups performed disappointingly because after three years the grants ran out and the farmers discovered that it was possible to make a loss, so they pulled out. It is better organised now and the start-up grants have been increased. As time goes on the producers or groups should have more clout to arrange better deals with the large multiple stores who take a great deal of the produce.

CAP and GATT - what of the future? I am rather more bullish than most people about the future. GATT with all its warts has been agreed, and no one is likely to interfere with its conclusions with the possible exception of the Americans. The CAP agreement guarantees farmers an income on arable payments until the end of 1996 - so all the opportunity it offers to make money and reduce overdrafts should be taken. The milk quotas are guaranteed until the year 2000. I believe that will be honoured as we are still short of full capacity.

What I believe will happen is that, with a rising world population, all food will be required, so by tinkering about with set-aside and allowing non-subsidised crops, which are already in surplus, to be used for commercial uses, eg OSR for fuel, wheat for industrial alcohol and timber products for biomass, full production could again be the goal to aim for. There will be constraints and all will be of a conservation nature or environmentally acceptable. The most damaging could be the reduction in livestock numbers. This will be coupled with the reduction in farms, because farms are and will continue to become larger. All I ask for is that proper countrymen, not 'green' freaks, are allowed to formulate any future changes.

If my prophesy is as correct as the following article, written over 100 years ago by W. Bromley Davenport, I would not be happy about the future.

But Who Shall Pierce The Veil Of The Future?

But who shall pierce the veil of the future? As with individuals, so I think it is with nations. They too when they grow old should preserve, or at least not too remorselessly extinguish, their follies. I fear lest in grasping at the shadow of national perfection we only attain the reality of a saturnalia of prigs - an apotheosis of claptrap. Legislation has performed such queer antics lately that the angels must be beginning to weep. And ugly visions sometimes haunt me of a time coming, which shall be a good time to no man, at least to no Englishman, when an impossible standard of pseudophilanthropy and humanitarian morality shall be tempted; when the butchers shall lie down with the lamb, the alderman with the turtle, and the oyster shall not be eaten without anaesthetics; when nature itself shall be under the eye of the police, and detectives watch the stoat's pursuit of the rabbit and keep guard over spiders' webs; when all property (and not in land alone, my advanced friend!) save that of Hardware magnates, who have made a monopoly and called it peace, shall be confiscated as an 'unearned increment' to the State; when we have by legislative enactment forbidden the prevention and sanctioned the admission of loathsome diseases, and anti-foxhunting may be as loud a cry as anti-vaccination; when there is a Parliament on College Green; when the 'languishing nobleman' of Dartmoor is free, and repossessed of his broad acres, which, in this case alone, because they so clearly belong to someone else, shall escape confiscation; when, as a final climax to our national madness, we have employed science to dig a hole under the sea, and, by connecting us with the Continent, deprive us of the grand advantage which nature has given us, and which has conferred on us centuries of envied stability, while thrones were rocking and constitutions sinking all around us; when, having already passed laws not only to prohibit our children being educated with the knowledge and fear of God before their eyes, but even to forbid his very name to be mentioned in our schools, we deliberately and scornfully abandon our ancient religion and admit proclaimed infidelity and public blasphemy to the sanction, recognition and approval of Parliament; then indeed we need not wonder if we lose not only our national sports, but our national existence; and in Divine Providence, giving practical effect to the old quotation,

Quos Deus vult perdere prius dementat.
What God wishes to lose he fast forgets.

allows England, after passing through the phases of insanity which she has already begun to display, to be blotted out from the nations of the world.

APPENDIX 1.
THE NEED AND MEANS OF INCREASING SELF-SUFFICIENCY ON THE FARM

by R. A. Hamilton

Note

I make no apologies for including Bob Hamilton's paper at the Farmers' Club on 7 April 1952, the year and the date that I moved up to The Leaths. I missed the occasion, which was a pity, for upon reading it the other day I realised that it was written about results in 1950 when I was the Farm Manager there, and it is the best example of our work during the time he was Director. From reading the paper you will see that he was an entirely dedicated man who put his heart and soul into everything he did. He was a wonderful boss and one who by sheer example could get the best out of those who worked for him. He was tough and single-minded, but was always fair and defended us lesser mortals through thick and thin if we were right.

Bob Hamilton even trusted me with the pre-farming training of his second son, who was obviously born before his time, as his idea of bedding cattle yards with straw was to cut the strings, remove them, then chase the cattle round to spread it. I caught him at it and was furious. It is now common practice.

His boss, Lord Fleck, who became Chairman of ICI, was another good friend to me and always came to see what I was up to if he was in the area. He wrote every Christmas, even after he had retired, and he took an interest until he died.

I was lucky to work with two such wonderful people who left me alone for 23 years, doing what I knew best. I knew one man who told me that he was selling fertilisers one morning, and had his job changed to another Division and was selling zip fasteners the following day.

'THE NEED AND MEANS OF INCREASING SELF-SUFFICIENCY ON THE FARM'
by
R. A. HAMILTON, BSc, B Agr, Dip Agric (Cantab), AICTA

A MEETING OF THE FARMERS' CLUB WAS HELD IN THE HALL OF THE ROYAL EMPIRE SOCIETY ON MONDAY, 7 APRIL 1952, AT 2.15 pm. MR H. R. OVERMAN WAS IN THE CHAIR.

The Chairman: We have with us today Mr Hamilton, who is to read a paper which, I can see from the large audience, has tickled the palate of a great many of you.

Mr Hamilton, of the Imperial Chemical Industries, was brought up on a farm in Northern Ireland. After leaving school he won a scholarship to Greenmount Agricultural College, Northern Ireland, followed by four years' scholarship at Queens University, Belfast. He graduated with first class honours and was awarded a two years' Colonial Agricultural Scholarship to Cambridge and the Imperial College of Tropical Agriculture, etc, etc. I could not possibly find time to give you a detailed list of his achievements and qualifications. In other words, we are to have a paper by someone who is somebody. Since 1944 Mr Hamilton has been the Development Director, Central Agricultural Control, of the Imperial Chemical Industries, and he is responsible for his company farms in Somerset, Cheshire, Kirkcudbrightshire and Durham, totalling some 3,000 acres.

May I say that I received a letter this morning from our Vice-President, Lord Bledislow, who wrote the following about the paper: 'If only I could have been present I should have claimed for 5 minutes the indulgence of my valued Farmers' Club colleagues to endorse emphatically the salutary gospel that Mr Hamilton will be preaching. His paper will, in my opinion, rank high in the literature of the Club as an epoch-making address. What he is saying today will, I feel sure, be recognised in its main features by 90 per cent of our successful practitioners ten years hence as incontrovertible wisdom.'

To propose a vote of thanks we have Mr A. S. Cray, who farmed in Wiltshire until 1922, when he joined one of the national dairy companies, and has been with them ever since. Since 1940 he has farmed at Medstead in Hampshire. He has had experiences of grassland improvement and intensive management. He supervises three mixed farms in Dorset,

Cornwall and Carmarthenshire, totalling 1,300 acres for the dairy company.

This morning, when I was in the club, I received a message from Mr Alexander's secretary saying that Mr Alexander was unfortunately unable to be present this afternoon. However, very gallantly my old friend Mr Roland Dudley has stepped into the breach to second the vote of thanks.

It now gives me pleasure to call on Mr Hamilton to read his paper.

* * *

I would consider it an honour to be asked to address the Club at any time, but to be invited to address you on today's subject is to me an added privilege and responsibility.

I say this because I believe there is a great and urgent need to increase agricultural self-sufficiency, both nationally and on the individual farm.

It seems to me that British agriculture has reached one of the most important points in its history.

We have already been told that we must have a larger agricultural industry than that envisaged in the expansion programme of 1947 - many well-informed people believe that it must be very much larger.

Is this because of the latest economic crisis? I don't think so - I am convinced that the need to produce more food at home will continue long after we have overcome the latest balance of payments crisis: that is, if the people of this country are to have a proper diet with the meat they have been used to in the past. There are those who say that we shall not have the meat, and that we must become largely vegetarians and accept a low standard of nutrition. Few will agree with this view. We hear much of the need to increase industrial productivity, but miners will not hew much coal on leeks and lettuce - however much they value the leek on occasions. Addressing you some seven years ago, a distinguished economist - Geoffrey Crowther - while supporting a home agricultural industry of about the size it was in 1938, advanced the classical economic argument that we can get most food per man-hour out of British labour by expending it to manufacturers, exporting them and buying our food abroad. He went on to say that we should be able to buy from abroad quite quickly - say in two years - most things that matter in food imports. Seven years have passed, and in important categories of food we are worse off than ever!

I am not an economist, and I hesitate to question an argument that has held sway for so long, but I believe there is good evidence to show that this classical economic argument is crashing about our ears, and that in relation to most other industries in Britain the agricultural industry is advancing in importance.

In other words, if we want a leg of lamb or a roast of pork, I suggest we have a better chance to getting it in future from a man-hour spent on a combine harvester in Wiltshire than in a car factory in Coventry.

Of course, we make for export and sell abroad all the industrial products we possibly can - in order to pay for raw materials and some food imports - but in the opinion of many well-informed and far-sighted people, we shall never again be able to depend on imported food to the extent we have done for the past hundred years.

Look around the world! What countries are going to have the food surpluses - especially meat products - to sell us? Very few. And many of the overseas countries which previously were engaged in food production for exports are now making their own industrial goods and no longer need to export so much food in exchange for industrial goods in Britain. The increasing industrialisation and rising standards of living in the great primary producing countries have made Britain extremely vulnerable as regards food imports, and the sooner our people realise this and come out in full support of a policy of maximum production of food at home, the better.

We sometimes hear of rosy prospects of obtaining food in quantity from the great undeveloped lands, mostly in the Tropics. I happen to have specialised in the study of tropical soils at one period, and I can assure you that, so far as the humid Tropics are concerned, their soils are among the poorest in the world - the luxuriance of the tropical rain forest as a guide to soil fertility is as deceptive as a mirage in the desert. Many problems will need to be solved before we can hope for more food from these areas. In fact, most of the great undeveloped areas in the Tropics will find it difficult to feed their own populations.

Before the war Britain produced one-third of her food and imported two-thirds. In the new world conditions, it is my view that we shall have to produce in future at least two-thirds of our food and import not more than one-third. Mr Chairman, I submit that there is a great need nationally to increase self-sufficiency in food production.

Can this great need be met? We have got the soil, we have got the climate, it would be possible to provide the raw materials - have we got the will to meet the need? If we haven't, millions will go hungry, and where will industrial production be then?

If we decide to join in this fight against a declining diet, how best can we increase self-sufficiency in food production? There seems no doubt that the major need is more meat. More beef, more lamb and mutton, and more pig meat.

Can more meat be produced? I propose to show that it can - provided that the British farmer can feel assured of a continuing demand for his output at a price which will give him a reasonable return. If the arguments of the classical economists no longer apply, it is clear that the farmer can be confident of an assured and lasting demand, and it remains for me to suggest how he should set out meeting it.

By far the biggest job is to provide more feed for the livestock. Of all the basic food produced from the soil of Britain today from both crops and grass, more than 80 per cent is consumed by livestock. If we keep more animals, we shall need even more animal feed, and we must provide this feed from home resources. It would be fatal from the start to build up increased herds on uncertain imports.

Can we provide the feeding stuffs necessary for any envisaged expansion of livestock from home resources? My answer is yes, and at far lower costs than feeding-stuffs obtained from any other source.

I have been associated with an investigation over the past few years in which detailed records are kept of output and costs on some 60 farms mainly concerned with dairying, and I would like to discuss some of the data which we have obtained from these farms.

Table 1

Estimated cost of starch equivalent from various crops in 1950 and dairy cake

Crop	Cost of starch equivalent (£ per ton)	Relative cost grazing = 100	
Section A			
Grazing (effective production)	8.5	100	Section A contains
Grass silage	18	212	the more firmly based
Hay	19	224	estimates taken from
Dried grass	31	365	the farms on which
Oats, straw fed	20	235	full cost accounts
Kale, cut	22	259	are kept.
Arable silage	33	388	
Mangolds	37	435	
Section B			
'Early bite' (effective production)	12	141	Section B is more speculative - the
Kale, grazed	15	176	figures are drawn
'Extra' barley, half straw fed	25	294	from smaller samples with a greater degree
Fodder beet	23	271	of estimation.
Section C			
Dairy cake at £35 per ton	58	682	Section C is based on dairy cake at today's price.

Table 1 sets out the average costs of producing starch equivalent from various sources in 1950, and is in general self-explanatory.

As I have said, these are generally dairy farms, and in most part are situated in the western half of Great Britain. Few of them are specialists in arable production, so you will not expect low costs for arable crops, comparable with those on the highly mechanised arable farms.

The main points of this table are:

(1) As a source of starch equivalent, grass in all its forms is outstandingly cheap compared with purchased concentrates.

(2) Silage and hay are cheaper sources of starch equivalent than any other crops except grazed kale.

(3) Grass as grazing (normal or 'early bite') is by far the cheapest source of starch equivalent.

(4) Dried grass, while being a more expensive source of starch equivalent than other forms of grass, is still only slightly more than half the cost of dairy cake.

(5) Home-grown cereals, even on ordinary mixed dairy farms, are less than half the cost of purchased feed.

(6) Roots, while dearer than grass and cereals, are high-yielding, and such crops as kale grazed and fodder beet seem very promising as regards cost.

From this table it is clear that it will pay well to go all-out to obtain the feeding-stuffs for the increased meat production from home resources - we must do this is two ways:

(1) Increase the self-sufficiency of our stock farms.

(2) Expand to the limit the production of mobile stock feed from the arable farms - the cost of coarse grains from arable farms will compare even more favourably with imported feed than those from the dairy farms listed above.

MEANS OF INCREASING SELF-SUFFICIENCY

The broad means of increasing self-sufficiency in livestock feed is best looked at according to type of livestock. In the time available to me, however, I cannot go into great detail.

Beef and mutton

For increased production of beef, mutton and lamb, grass in its cheapest form - grazing - must be the main - indeed, almost the sole - source of feed.

The value of good grass and beef production is, of course, well known. This subject was fully covered by Mr Passmore when he addressed the Club last month.

I only propose to enlarge on a few points:

(1) By the application of modern methods of grassland management, output of beef per acre can be increased substantially from all but the best fattening pastures. While not always applicable, it has shown that the strip grazing technique developed for dairy cows can also be used to advantage for beef production.

(2) A large quantity of grass which is grown at present is not fully utilised, and there are good grounds for believing that much of this could be used profitably by sheep, especially in late autumn and winter, without reducing the grass available for dairy cows or other cattle.

(3) Grass as grazing, or conserved as hay, silage and dried grass, can provide all of the requirements of store stock in winter. Recent work in the Grassland Research Station and elsewhere holds out promise for providing some winter grazing by specially managing grass fields in summer and shutting them up for use in winter.

(4) Experiments on fattening cattle wholly or partially on grass silage in winter have shown this to be one of the most profitable methods of winter fattening, although it is still, of course, much more expensive than summer fattening off grass.

Can we, then, produce enough grass to carry the extra stock necessary to provide the additional beef and mutton required? Without doubt technically we could increase grassland output by 25 per cent, and this would be equivalent to over 4 million tons of coarse grains.

By a more general adoption of ley farming, still higher production would be economically possible. I shall return to this point later.

Pigs

Grass in quantity is not a suitable feed for fattening pigs, and for pigs we must produce more coarse grains - home-produced coarse grains being much cheaper than imported.

We can do this in two ways:

(1) By increasing the acreage under cereals - some steps have already been taken in this direction. Ploughing up more old grass for cereals is not in any way incompatible with increasing production from grassland - indeed, it will assist it by bringing a larger area eventually into the ley system.

(2) By increasing the yield of the present coarse grain acreage. It is estimated that if modern techniques of production were applied to all cereals, yields could be increased by 10 per cent. What an effect on total production this would be - at least an extra 500,000 tons! Surely the time has come when every acre of arable land, in addition to being well tilled, should be given the best chance of yielding a full crop by using:

The right variety
The right fertiliser
The right protection against pests, diseases and weeds

Anything less than 100 per cent adoption of the best techniques is false economy.

For pigs many people have high hopes of fodder beet, and of course this is the mainstay of Danish production at present and largely makes good their loss of imported feeding-stuffs. At one of our farms this year, one acre of fodder beet produced 22 tons of beet per acre of 20 per cent dry matter - nearly 4½ tons per acre, not counting tops.

Increased production of coarse grains is not the only means of obtaining additional concentrates for pigs. By using grass to a greater extent for milk production, some concentrates now fed to dairy cows could be released for pigs and poultry. Indeed, more efficient use of grass for milk production in winter and summer could release as much concentrates for pigs and poultry as would be grown by ploughing another million acres for cereals.

Milk

No one would expect the dairy farmer to go to the trouble of changing his methods to increase his dependence on grass and use less concentrates merely to release them for pigs and poultry unless there were something in it for him. In the case of most dairy farms there would, in fact, be substantial advantage.

From Table 1 it is clear that the more grass that can be used to feed cows, the cheaper will be the feeding costs, compared with those of purchased cake. Indeed, it might seem that provided milk yields can be maintained, cows should be fed entirely on grass. The fallacy in this argument is that although cost of feed per cow would fall, the number of cows which could be kept would fall too, unless on the average dairy farm there would be a substantial rise in output from the grassland; in general, it would need to be doubled.

For most farms, therefore, there must be an optimum level at which grass can be used for milk production, and I suggest that the optimum level is substantially higher than the present level, and that one of the readiest means of increasing profitability of milk production is to increase the proportion of grass in the diet of the dairy cow.

At present I estimate that:

(1) The average effective production from grassland on dairy farms in the UK is about 15 cwt starch equivalent per acre.

(2) The national dairy herd relies on grass in its various forms for less than 50 per cent of its total food needs.

(3) About 3 to 4 lbs of concentrates (purchased and home-grown) are fed to cows for every gallon of milk produced by the national dairy herd worth an average milk yield of about 600 gallons per cow. This seems to be an unnecessary, indeed uneconomic, use of a very expensive commodity.

The problem, then, is to increase grass production on the average dairy farm above 15 cwt starch equivalent per acre, to raise the percentage of grass and grass products in the feed of the dairy herd above 55 per cent, and to reduce the amount of concentrates fed appreciably below 3 to 4 lbs per gallon of milk produced. Can this be done in such a way that milk yield will not fall - or at least so that any reduction in yield will be more than compensated for by a reduction in cost of feeding - ie so that profit per cow will increase? This is an important question, and my answer to it is yes.

With the exception of farms on which advanced grassland husbandry is already being practised, most dairy farms could with profit increase the percentage of grass in the feeding of their cows.

The first need will be to increase actual yields of grass, and there is no question that even on moderate or moderately poor land on the western half of Britain grass yields could be increased 25 per cent or more. I do not have time to submit evidence or suggest means by which this can be done at this stage, but it is certain that it can be done.

The extent to which grass can be substituted for concentrates will, of course, vary. Some farms, mainly the larger ones, will be able to go a very long way in this direction. We have records of some very successful dairy farms with equal summer and winter production, where grass forms over 90 per cent of the total feed for dairy cows. Others, mainly very small, heavily stocked, specialised dairy farms, some on poor land, will not be able to go nearly so far, but there is no doubt that they can improve their position by intensifying grass production. Indeed, there is urgent need for the smaller farms to become more intensive in grass production than any other farms in the country - we have records of some such farms where grass forms over 70 per cent of total feed.

For the group of 60 farms that I have already mentioned, in the year 1950 grass and grass products provided about 65 per cent of the total ration. The average milk yield* per cow in the combined herds was 710 gallons, and the average income from milk £102 per cow in the herd - a substantial proportion of the milk having been produced in winter. Some of these are small farms on moderate land - indeed, some of them are in areas like East Lancs and the West Riding and in Wales at altitudes of up to 1,000 feet.

. . .Recently Mr Kenneth Russell gave you a very interesting paper on 'Dairy Herd Management', and in his address he tended to put a limit on the value of grass for milk production, especially in winter, very much lower than I have suggested. Mr Russell based his opinion mainly on the belief that high reliance on grass, except during a limited period in summer, necessarily means uneconomically low yields per cow. To achieve the level of milk yield advocated by Mr Russell would surely require a quantity of concentrates for cows far in excess of anything which can be supplied - and at what a cost! By using far less concentrates than the national average, however, and far more grass, the above farms have achieved higher milk yields than the national average and made a good profit per cow per acre.

The fact that grass can sustain reasonably high milk yields is, of course, shown in New Zealand - the lowest-cost milk-producer in the world. However, New Zealand has a very long grazing season and produces mainly summer milk, and is not therefore a fair comparison with this country.

Take Holland - a country nearer home with a shorter grazing season than our own. Holland relies on grass for over 80 per cent of her milk production, yet she has the highest national herd average in the world and is probably, with Denmark, the lowest-cost producer of milk in Europe, or, with the exception of New Zealand, in the world.

Mr Chairman, on the evidence now available, I feel I am justified in claiming that we can substantially increase self-sufficiency through grass on the dairy farm, and at the same time cut the cost of feeding - by far the most expensive item in milk production today.

INCREASING THE OUTPUT FROM GRASSLAND

This, of course, is a subject in itself, and I shall only have time to refer briefly to some of the more important aspects of it.

It will be obvious from the extent to which I have said we must rely on grass for milk and beef production that we shall have to achieve a consid-

* Total production divided by the average weekly number of cows and heifers in milk and dry cows.

erable increase in the output from our grasslands. Let us first of all be quite clear what we mean by increased output from grassland.

There is a vast difference between increasing output from grassland and increasing production of grass. I judge the output of a grass field by recording the production of animal products - milk, meat, mutton, etc - calculating how much food, usually in terms of starch equivalent, was needed to get this production of animal products, and subtracting from this the value of any other feeding-stuffs fed to the animals. For comparative purposes this gives me the best measure I know of grassland output or grassland productivity.

Output therefore depends on:

(1) The amount of grass grown.

(2) The amount of the grass that is eaten by the stock.

(3) The feeding quality of the grass.

(4) The efficiency of the stock in converting the grass.

In other words, high output from grassland depends on growing good grass and making the best use of it.

The proper use of grass is of such importance that, in deciding on a policy of increased grassland productivity, plans to make the best use of the grass must always take precedence over steps to increase yield.

It is useless to spend money on increasing grass yields and then waste a large proportion of the grass. On the other hand, if good use is to be made of the grass, it is well worth while taking steps to increase it production. Further, I suggest that the degree of increased production should be in step with the degree of efficiency of utilisation - any other approach leads not only to waste, but possibly also to damage to swards and disappointment.

This I am sure, will seem elementary to many of you, but it is my view that few farms in the country today make the best use of the grass they grow.

Making good use of grass

The aim should always be to grow a good crop of grass and then harvest it at the right time with the minimum waste, with:

(1) The grazing animal, or

(2) Strip grazing, which also offers the animal a better-balanced diet and thus tends towards steadier milk yields and less digestive trouble. To obtain full advantage from strip grazing it should be alternated with cutting.

Hay

(1) While silage-making and grass-drying are more efficient forms of conservation in most grasslands districts, a quantity of good hay is still always valuable. The whole aim must be to make *good* hay, however, and one of the best ways will be on tripods - a method that can provide hay containing on the average 3 to 4 per cent more protein than hay made by most methods.

(2) The second best way to make good hay is to make much less of it. A moderate quantity of good hay and a substantial quantity of good silage is under present conditions much more valuable than a large quantity of indifferent hay.

Silage

(1) The aim in silage-making has generally been to have a fairly high protein content. Recent experience suggests that the more important aim should be a high dry-matter content. High-protein and low-dry-matter silage is less valuable than high-dry-matter and modern protein silage.

    To obtain high-dry-matter silage it is necessary to ensure that the green material going into the silo is not too wet, and that where a pit silo is used it is properly sited for drainage.

(2) It now seems doubtful whether in most parts of the British Isles it is possible to produce high-dry-matter silage without a weatherproof covering. The most urgent need in pit silage-making is to find convenient and cheap weatherproof cover.

    On fields intended for 'early bite', its effects will be to carry over some growth till spring, which will be more fibrous as 'early bite' and as a result may make a better diet than very young, lush grass.

(3) The application of nitrogen to fields to be cut for hay, silage or drying ten days to a fortnight before cutting in nearly all cases substantially increases the crude protein content of the grass, and the increase is nearly all as digestible protein. There is usually no effect on yield of that cut, but the swards recover quickly and the next growth benefits. Recent experiments suggest that very high yields of high-protein grass can be obtained by this technique.

(4) While nitrogen is most valuable on grass in the early and late season, there is need for nitrogen on some fields on most farms throughout the season. This varies with climatic conditions, but it would seem that in the South West there is less need for nitrogen in the middle part of the season than there is further North.

Type of sward and the use of nitrogen

It is sometimes said that nitrogen depresses or kills out clovers. This is not strictly true. Nitrogen encourages grasses, and if the quantities are large and the management is such that the grasses become very vigorous and tall, the clovers are often suppressed or killed out because of their inability to compete with the well-fed grasses. Clovers, however, contribute substantial amounts of nitrogen to swards, and the maximum advantage should be taken of this fact. It does not follow, however, that grass should always be managed with a view to maintaining a high clover content.

In New Zealand and Holland, the leading grassland countries in the world, distinctly opposite values are placed on clover. In the former it is of the utmost importance - in the latter it is practically ignored, especially on the good grassland farms.

I suggest that our position is somewhat intermediate between these two, and in my experience the following should be a useful guide to the use of nitrogen on different types of sward:

(a) *H I Ryegrass short-rotation ley*
     This ley is not worth sowing unless nitrogen is used liberally. If 5-10 cwt per acre of 'Nitro-chalk' is used, this ley will produce heavily, and early and late, and total production over the season could always be over 3 tons dry matter to the acre - sometimes over 4 tons. Much of this is produced when other fields are bare.

     With this ley it is not vital to retain clover, but even with such high level production 2 lb S.100 white clover seems worthwhile, and it is surprising how it persists.

(b) *Timothy/meadow fescue/white clover, timothy/meadow fescue/white cocksfoot/white clover, cocksfoot/white clover and similar leys*
     These leys make the most important contribution during midsummer, when ryegrasses are not productive. With these leys it is essential to maintain a high clover content, and heavy dressings of nitrogen should be used only in special cases.

     If no nitrogen is used, however, they tend to become very clovery and the good grasses die out as they are not adequately fed. This may give rise to digestive and other troubles in stock.

     Moderate dressings of nitrogen, 2-4 cwt per acre, will maintain a better grass/clover balance and increase yield.

(c) *Cockle Park-type leys and special-purpose leys based on perennial ryegrass*
     In so far as the need for nitrogen is concerned, these leys are, I think, intermediate between (a) and (b). The clover content should be maintained at a reasonable level, but the ryegrass will not be productive, or as early as it should be, unless fertiliser nitrogen is used. Dressings of 2-6 cwt nitrogen fertiliser can be used according to conditions.

(d) *Permanent pasture*

Even though it may contain some white clover, the bulk of the permanent pasture of this country is relatively unproductive unless manured with nitrogen. Properly manured, even moderate-quality permanent pasture in the high rainfall districts can become quite productive and can provide feed at very low cost. Anything from 2 to 6 cwt nitrogen fertiliser yearly is essential for good production.

Based on records obtained for output of grass from a number of fields over recent years, I suggest that nitrogen used as described above will increase effective grass production by 25 to 50 per cent. Further, we find that the protein content of the grass is on the average increased by about one-fifth, and the grazing season is normally substantially extended.

The quantities of fertilisers which have been used in practice on all the grassland on 54 of the commercial farms to which I referred earlier are shown in Table 2.

What grassland can do

I have mentioned that the average utilised starch equivalent production from grass on dairy farms in the UK is of the order of 15 cwt per acre.

By applying some of the techniques and principles that I have discussed, levels of production from grass have been obtained on several of the commercial farms on which we are working equivalent to over 20 cwt utilised starch equivalent per acre over the whole farm.

In 1949 20 cwt was exceeded on 14 of the farms, including a 70-acre farm carrying 40 cows on very moderate land above 1,000 feet in the West

	Average acres grass	'Nitro-chalk'	Super phosphate	Muriate of potash
	Table 2			
	1949 cwt per acre			
25 farms over 150 acres	214	1.3	1.4	0.2
29 farms under 150 acres	64	2.0	2.7	0.3
	1950 cwt per acre			
25 farms over 150 acres	204	2.0	1.8	0.3
29 farms under 150 acres	68	3.0	2.5	0.4

Riding. In 1950 it was exceeded on 25 of the farms, and we are expecting that several more will have exceeded 20 cwt in 1951.

In 1950 seven of the farms exceeded 25 cwt per acre. This would be equivalent to a yield of 35 cwt barley per acre over the whole farm, every ounce of which gave its full theoretical value when fed to animals.

On Dairy House 'A' farm of 185 acres output was 32 cwt starch equivalent per acre - equivalent to 46 cwt barley efficiently used from every acre. This is one of the highest figures ever recorded for a whole farm.

This is what grass can do, Mr Chairman - and if we add to what we can get from properly managed grass the extra production that is possible from applying the best techniques to our arable crops, can anyone doubt that we could provide two-thirds of our food requirements - and more? I will go further - if we were to decide on a long-term policy to produce two-thirds of our food needs, and we base this on getting most of our feed for cattle and sheep by efficient use of our grasslands, and on getting full yields from an increased acreage of arable crops, I am certain that more economical production of food could be achieved in the long run.

CONCLUSION

Mr Chairman, in conclusion I submit that there is need - urgent need - to increase self-sufficiency on the farm. I am equally sure that we have the means at hand. Let us hope - indeed resolve - that we will use them before it is too late.

Appendix 2.
Experimental Farm Run on Commercial Basis

A look round The Leaths

The farming scene
by Robert Urquhart

(Article in *The Scotsman*, Saturday 2 July 1960)

There is nothing more fascinating for a farmer than to have a close look at another man's farm - '. . .the grass is always greener on the other side of the hill . . .' - but even more fascinating, to my mind, are the farms which help themselves and other farmers to farm better by enquiring into or developing new techniques.

The Leaths at Castle Douglas, owned by Imperial Chemical Industries Ltd, is one of these farms, but there is one point about it that must be taken right beyond the line of argument for a start, and that is that, while this is an experimental farm, it is also run on a completely commercial basis.

This should make it quite impossible for the average farmer, who may find himself there and looking at some of the things which will open his eyes, to say: 'It's all very well for them here. They're ICI.' I say it should make it impossible for farmers to say that - but it won't stop them saying it!

Nevertheless, it is a fact that on this highly organised holding the fact that it provides a testing ground for ideas does not mean that it should not make a profit, for it most certainly does. Indeed, at The Leaths the value of any scheme, method or practice is judged finally by the acid test of profitability.

MOST IMPORTANT FACTOR

The more reconnaissances I make to see how the battle goes on the farming front, the more I am convinced that the most important single factor in successful farming is the farmer himself. I know that the soil, the organisation, the climate, the altitude, the aspect, the bigness or the smallness, the slope or lack of it, and a host of other physical factors have their impact on the success or otherwise of the enterprise, but the vital one is the man.

I do not say this because I happened to meet Mr Peter Maclaren, The Leaths's manager, for the first time. It is just that in meeting him - and I have met others like him - this point about the importance of the man in charge seemed to be driven home so forcefully.

There is so much to write about The Leaths that this Saturday causerie can do no more than touch on just a few points. Started first of all as a dairy farm, at least in the main, it later developed other enterprises such as sheep, barley growing (a development that has led to a lot more barley being grown in the district) and, more recently, beef cattle - that is beef from the dairy herd. The beef project was started, not because it was thought that it would be more profitable than milk, but because of the flood of milk and the need for more beef it was felt that much more information was required on the profitability of beef from the dairy herd.

At The Leaths two men manage 120 dairy cows, which is a sufficiently startling thing to start off with. I may be wrong, but I should say that on many other farms in the South West it would take three or more to do this.

VAST AMOUNT OF SILAGE

There is, needless to say, a vast amount of silage made. One might have thought that an organisation so interested in grass, and especially the means of making it grow, would be thinking of zero grazing, but perhaps that would not give enough scope for the need for diversification of research enterprise as the farm tests new fertilisers, weed-killers and animal heath remedies produced by ICI.

Above all, it is fully costed, so exactly, as was jokingly remarked, that they know how much it costs for the manager to walk across the farmyard.

Other investigations are on soil fertility, technical records on grass, crop and milk production and the health of stock and the weather conditions.

Any one of these or half a dozen other aspects of the work here would provide at least one good, soil technical article, but I went for a combination farm walk and a general look-see.

GRASS IS GREAT

Understandably, the grass is great, but that does not mean that in experiments a mistake or two has not been made, not only on grass but on the bringing up of the big herd of 150 beef stores. These mistakes have been signposts, not stumbling blocks, to progress.

While I marvelled at the hugh tonnages of silage - 1,500 tons is the normal annual requirement - on the management of the big sheep flock and beef cattle herd, I was no less struck by the examples of local ingenuity and ability which were also to be seen.

This last point is as important as any for, while a farmer must be a strategist and plan ahead, he must also surmount many tactical problems. For instance, at The Leaths there was this matter of the milk records and the costing of staffing or whatever you like to call it.

MICROPHONE MILK

Recording milk by the usual methods did demand labour and time, so Mr Maclaren installed flow meters which measured the flow and therefore the quantity of the milk to 97 per cent accuracy, which was good enough for his purposes - but that still meant someone writing records. So he fixed a microphone or two near the flow meters, and led the line to a tape-recorder.

Now, as the cows came in and are milked, the flow is read and the cow's number and performance are spoken into the mike and the information dealt with by the young lady in the office. This cuts out a lot of time-wasting measuring of milk and writing on the spot.

There was also the fascinating matter of the three-way gates. By the simple lifting of a pin and putting it in another socket, the hinge end of the gate is changed, or the gate is locked in a direction. In the handling of stock, little gadgets like this are as valuable as an able-bodied human.

BUSINESS OF BEEF

The most recent development is, of course, this business of beef from the dairy herd. It has little more than begun, and has already thrown up a lot of interesting information - and animals. The products may look just slightly on the small side, but they do look good as beef stock and they have in fact been admired, and some purchased, by one of the acknowledged experts in this method of getting more beef into the larder.

The daily weight gains of these animals on grass were quite fantastic, and there is no doubt that the work The Leaths is doing on these lines will provide a lot of information. Here again the whole job will be costed, and one of the things we really need about beef is detailed costings. We have had costings, but we are going to need more of the kind that The Leaths is doing to clarify the picture even more.

PLENTY OF ADVICE

Mention of costing again brings me to this matter of the importance of the person of the farmer or of the manager. In view of the vast amount of advice that is available, it would almost seem that a great number of quite good farmers are still stone-blind as to how they should really go about their business. In British farming today advice is available on every single aspect of the industry and where doubt about local application exists, that, too, can be met.

It is places like The Leaths which make this volume of available information not only more complete year by year but improve its quality - while still running along as a highly successful commercial farm.

APPENDIX 3.
FIELD DAY AT THE LEATHS

(Article in the *Galloway News*, June 1961)

Agriculturalists from many parts of Scotland to the number of 514 spent an interesting and highly profitable day on Tuesday at the 468-farm of The Leaths, Castle Douglas, belonging to the ICI, the event being arranged by their associate enterprise, Scottish Agricultural Industries Ltd. This large farm is expertly managed by Mr N. P. Maclaren.

It was pointed out in the course of the day's proceedings that The Leaths is one of the three ICI demonstration farms devoted to exploring ways and means of making the fullest possible use of grass in the production of milk, mutton and beef, thereby reducing costs and increasing profits.

In this connection it was emphasised by several of the principal speakers that a planned system of grassland management is vital to the national economy of Britain and would inevitably lead to a prosperous and efficient agriculture throughout the country.

It was also indicated that The Leaths was not purely a commercial enterprise, but figures produced at the forenoon conference revealed a steadily expanding economy, with sales of produce soaring and expenditure steadily declining.

A hugh marquee situated in a field opposite the main steading was fully occupied for the morning conference, and a pleasant note was struck by the promoters in garlanding the base of the platform with hydrangea and other attractive blooms.

CLOSELY RELATED

The chair was occupied by Mr R. A. Hamilton, a Director of the Billingham Division ICI, who extended a cordial welcome to the 500-odd guests. Mr Hamilton said that he decided in 1948 that ICI should buy the farm of The Leaths, and a little later was of the opinion it would be a very good idea if they could get Peter Maclaren to run it. He was very proud that he had taken both these decisions.

The national economy of agriculture and grassland were in his view subjects that were fairly closely related. A prosperous and efficient agriculture was essential to the national economy of Britain, and a planned system of grassland management was necessary to achieve that end.

There were varying views about the importance of agriculture, and the present developments with regard to the Common Market did not make the subject any less complicated. He believed that a prosperous and efficient agriculture was absolutely essential to the wellbeing of the United Kingdom, and he believed it would continue to be so.

There was a tendency in the 'fifties for some people to take the view that they had got rid of their balance of payments difficulties and that perhaps a very big agriculture was not so important as in the previous 20 years. The advocates of such a proposal had quickly changed their minds.

In the 'forties it was necessary for them to get all the food they possibly could from the land in order that the people should not go hungry. That was equally necessary in the 'fifties in order that their economy should survive, because they had crisis on the financial front, and a balanced agriculture was necessary to help solve the many outstanding problems.

'I believe that in 1960 agriculture will be just as important, and I also believe that the balance of payments problem will always be with us'.

SERIOUS PLIGHT

Today agriculture in Britain was producing something like £1,600,000,000 worth of food per annum. No one had really suggested they should have a much smaller agriculture, but for the sake of argument let them assume someone decided they should reduce the size of British agriculture by 20 or 25 per cent. If that were done it would mean they would have to find food to the value of something like an additional £400,000,000 per year.

Last year their balance of payments deficiency came to about £300,000,000 and they got themselves into a really serious plight. No one could surely foresee a situation where they would have to reduce the size of agriculture by anything like that amount. In fact to be really sound they needed not a deficiency but a surplus of that amount.

The Common Market, of course, raised new problems. He did not know whether they should join the Common Market or not - he probably thought they would - but he did not believe British agriculture had anything to fear if they decided to do so. In fact, his view was that in the long run British agriculture would probably gain if they joined the Common Market, as their agriculture compared very favourably with that of most of the countries within the Common Market just now.

Their arable farming was probably just as good as the Netherlands, but the rate at which they produced grass and used fertilisers in the grass was appreciably above ours. Western Germany, which had an agriculture extent about the size of Britain, was perhaps not so efficient, but it was more heavily subsidised.

The management of grass in the national economy was very important for a very simple reason, that it was the cheapest form of livestock feed. Farmers who managed their own grass would make a bigger profit than those who did not. The Leaths farm formed part of a general scheme in the development work undertaken by ICI and SAI for the past ten years or so. The main reason for the scheme was a belief by those two companies that the whole development of the grassland of Britain would contribute probably more than almost any other single factor to increased agricultural efficiency.

A PROFITABLE CONCERN

They co-operated with between 80 and 100 farmers throughout the country on farmland which was typical of the rest of the country. It was not the best land, neither was it the worst, but it was reasonably representative. Together they tried to decide ways and means of improving the efficiency of the farms through grass, and they costed them, which led to fairly clear-cut answers being given.

The conclusion had been reached that farmers who managed their own grassland would make about double the profit per acre as compared with those who worked at a general level, and on the farms operated by ICI in Scotland the figure would be even greater.

They did not run The Leaths farm purely on a commercial basis, but they ran it as a normal farm, introducing various techniques from time to time, and the results they got answered some difficult problems that might not be so easy to solve on a commercial farm.

Mr Hamilton pointed out that The Leaths was used as an experimental grassland agricultural farm. They would try anything there and see how it worked. Some things had worked well at The Leaths, particularly the self-feed silage system, but other things had not worked so well. They had by no means overcome all the problems, but we could say without fear of contradiction that The Leaths was very well farmed and that it was quite a profitable concern.

THE CHEAPEST FOOD

An interesting outline of the management of The Leaths was then given by Mr R. R. Turner, General Farms Manager of the ICI, who summarised the farming policy and cropping; buildings, labour and equipment; grassland, livestock and feeding systems used, the health of the stock and the production figures at The Leaths.

He mentioned that the farm was purchased by the ICI in 1948, and the total area was 506 acres, including 38 acres of waste ground, woods and building. The objective was to obtain maximum profit from stock and crops, and in doing so the returns from the greater use of fertilisers, particularly nitrogen on grassland, were investigated.

Grass, being the cheapest food, was utilised to the utmost for the production of milk, beef and mutton during the grazing season, and in winter self-fed silage played a very big part in the output of milk and beef.

A good pedigree Ayrshire herd was taken over with the farm, and milk production had been the main enterprise. A flock of some 250 ewes had been carried since 1953, and more recently ewes and lambs had been successfully grazed on a very intensive system, there being at present 280 ewes on the farm.

There was a change of policy in 1958 when, because of the national surplus of milk and scarcity of beef it was decided to produce the number of dairy cows and introduce beef production. Good type beef Shorthorn bulls were used to produce calves which were finished as beef at an early age using grass and silage, self-fed as far as possible.

REGULAR TESTS

During the summer the cow byres were cleared of standings for loose-housing, and two new covered sheds were built for silage self-feeding, while a new milking parlour was installed. As the number of beef cattle increased and the dairy herd, which averaged around 170 over the past ten years, had been reduced to 115, all of which could be comfortably housed, self-fed and looked after by two men.

No turnips had been grown since 1955, but a small acreage of kale was sown until 1959, when it was found that with adequate silage for self-feeding kale was unnecessary. Barley had gradually taken the place of oats because of its higher energy value, and the labour force consisted of seven men, compared with ten three years ago before the conversion to parlour milking and silage self-feeding.

The three silage sheds held about 400 tons each, and two cow byres housed 60 animals each.

APPENDIX 4.
AYRSHIRES CAN MAKE A USEFUL CONTRIBUTION TO BEEF SUPPLIES

Dairy herd experiments at The Leaths

Field day arouses wide interest

(Newspaper article)

About 300 agriculturists from all parts of Britain, with invited guests from South Africa, Australia, Holland and Ireland, watched a series of highly interesting demonstrations at The Leaths, Castle Douglas, farm of Imperial Chemicals Industries Ltd, on Tuesday forenoon, and later attended a conference at the Palace Cinema on the subject of beef production.

The major demonstration was arranged because of the widespread interest in beef production at the present time. Six years ago the herd of Ayrshire cows at The Leaths was reduced in order to introduce a beef from a dairy herd enterprise by using beef Shorthorn bulls on the Ayrshires. The invited guests saw the value of the cross for beef production, and the Institute of Meat had on display a wide range of carcases and joints from animals fattened on the farm.

It will be of interest to farmers generally to learn that of the 190 home-bred Shorthorn cross Ayrshire beef animals on the farm, 100 are in the fattening period, from calves to finishing, in 18 months. They and 96 purchased suckler calves are being fattened, mainly on silage, supplemented with barley and beet pulp.

SHORTAGE OF BEEF

Even the joints of meat at the luncheon in Castle Douglas Town Hall came from animals bred at The Leaths, and tribute was paid throughout the day to the exemplary organising abilities of Mr N. P. Maclaren, the manager, for the excellent arrangements made in connection with this field day, and for so ably supervising the demonstrations, etc.

The Leaths farm, which comprises a total of 506 acres and lies some 250 feet above sea level, is one of four British farms owned by ICI in Britain. The object of the farms is to evaluate new techniques and to demonstrate the technical and economic advantages of intensive systems.

An introduction to the forenoon series of demonstrations was the announcement that in the late 1950s there was in the United Kingdom a danger of an over-supply of milk and a shortage of beef. Since then, government incentives had encouraged beef production, and there has been a marked change in the type of beef in demand.

The housewife wants smaller, leaner joints, and these can be produced from animals slaughtered at about 18 months of age and weighing about 9 cwt. The present demand for calves for the production of increasing numbers of beef animals cannot be met by the beef and dual-purpose herds, with the result that an increasing number of beef cross calves from the national dairy herd are being used to meet the demand.

As early as 1957 the ICI decided to establish a beef enterprise at The Leaths, based on beef Shorthorn cross calves from the Ayrshire dairy cows. This had proved to be a far-sighted decision, particularly with the strong demand and favourable prices for beef at present.

With over 70 per cent of the beef produced in the country today coming directly or indirectly from dairy herds, in view of the performances at The Leaths it is clear that there is a bright future for the production of beef on this type.

SMITHFIELD HONOURS

The afternoon conference in the Palace Cinema was presided over by Mr R. A. Hamilton, Deputy Chairman of the ICI Agricultural Division, who was accompanied on the flowered-bedecked platform by the guest speaker, Professor Mac Cooper of Newcastle-on-Tyne and Mr Peter Maclaren.

Mr Hamilton mentioned that the conference was at one time in jeopardy because of the snowstorm. The subject of beef production was not only highly topical, but very important, and he felt it would continue to be so not only in the short term but also taking the long-term view.

They at The Leaths began seriously thinking about beef production around 1957. They had been very impressed, and, indeed, greatly encouraged in their plans to see some of the cattle which Mr James Biggar of Chapelton was getting from his Ayrshire cows crossed with his beef

Shorthorn bull. They were first-class cattle, and Mr Biggar did not use the worst of his bulls.

They were pleased to have Mr Biggar among their number that day, and they were all delighted at his recent success with his Galloways when he won the championship of the Smithfield Show in London and had outstanding successes in his recent sales.

Introducing Professor Cooper, the Chairman said that he was Dean of the Faculty of Agriculture at Newcastle University, and was universally recognised as an international authority on the subject.

A LUXURY PRODUCT

Speaking on the important subject of beef from grass, Professor Cooper said he had been privileged to be at The Leaths when beef production started and now to see some of the effects of the Ayrshire Shorthorn calves that Mr Maclaren was rearing. That day's demonstrations came as something of a climax at a particularly appropriate time.

The housewives of Britain must realise that beef was a luxury product, and it was going to cost more. Indeed, when it was all added up, beef was a dear commodity to produce.

He mentioned that the Republic of Ireland was exporting more cattle to this country than ever before, something like 800,000 store cattle coming into Britain. He wondered how long that situation was going to continue before the Irish realised there was a market on the continent for finished cattle to suit continental needs, instead of a market for stores in this country.

The Professor said that barley beef, it seemed, was a luxury Britain could not afford. It here were no limitations on the supply of suitable calves, and there were large areas of land that could be switched to barley production, the system might have an expanding future.

But the simple fact was that they did not have enough calves to slaughter them at 7-8 cwt. When they had an economic potential of 9-10 cwt they were permitted to grow frame before they were finally finished at under 18 months of age.

With the first cwt of an animal costing £25 the rearer and feeder had no option but to spread this overhead over as many live cwts as he could, consistent with an economic return.

There was no better method of growing that frame economically than by the intensive use of grass, particularly with autumn-born calves. Perhaps the best commercial evidence to support that viewpoint had been provided by Mr Fenwick Jackson at his Kirkharle Farm in Northumberland. He showed very clearly that grass could not only grow frame but also, in the form of silage, could form the basis of the finishing diet. He found that silage alone, even though it was of high quality, was not an ideal finishing food. Very sensibly he supplemented it with barley to finish his animals by 18 months of age.

IMPORTANT CRITERION

They had further support for the system from the results that Mr Peter Maclaren had at The Leaths over the past five years, not with Friesians and their crosses but with the less favoured Shorthorn x Ayrshire calf as his raw material. Admittedly, he had not got the high finishing weights of the bigger breeds and crosses, but he had achieved a more important criterion, high live-weight gains per acre.

They could be over-concerned with high individual performance of stock if it was to the detriment of overall productivity of the farm, which could very well happen with the intensive utilisation of grass.

In that connection he liked The Leaths's approach to the use of grass for 6-12-month-old animals. They were not expected to make maximum live-weight gains while they were at pasture because such an objective would require a much lower stocking intensity.

The practical aim had been to use all the grass that was grown either as grazing or silage. During the height of the grazing season the calves were rotationally grazed at the rate of five to the acre.

Professor Cooper then dealt at length with the beef work at Cockle Park, where last summer 36 autumn-born Friesians grazed on 15 acres of grass. These grass-fed bullocks were going to give a net margin of at least £25 a piece while the barley beef steers they reared would have a margin of about £15.

Their experience indicated that it took about 1¼ acres of land to provide the nutriment required by an autumn-born calf from the three months stage to a final finishing weight of 9½ cwt at about 17 months of age. Of that area approximately two-thirds should be grass, to provide grazing and silage, with the balance in barley for supplementation.

It could not, however, be grass that was producing on 5,000-6,000 lbs of dry matter per acre, which was the practical limit when one was relying on clover nitrogen. It must be grass with a productivity of 7,500-8,000 lbs of dry matter - the sort of production one got from applying 180-200 units of nitrogen per acre - and it must be grass that was intensively utilised by rotational grazing and mowing.

MARGIN FROM GRASS

Admittedly, such a level of fertilising, and such a system of grazing, would not give them grass-fattened bullocks, but that was not the object. Prime finish at the end of the grazing season would demand a much lower intensity of grazing with set stocking and, of course, older bullocks, preferably of an early maturing beef cross. There they were concerned with a different proportion - the growth of frame in young cattle which were at the stage where they made the most economical use of food.

The value of their grass-reared bullocks at slaughter, including subsidy, was at least £90 a piece which, on that intensity of land use, gave a gross return of £75 per acre. If they put the all-in cost of producing grass and barley at £25 per acre, and put the cost of the three-month calf at £35, they had a margin of at least £22 per acre to cover bedding, veterinary costs, additional labour and overheads.

These, with a reasonable scale of enterprise, would not amount to more than £7 per acre, to leave a balance of £15 which constituted a clear profit.

For those who argued the danger of basing commercial estimates on experimental data, he would point to the gross margin of £38 that The Leaths had been achieving from its grass. He was reasonably certain that represented a net margin of at least £20 per acre - and that with Ayrshire crosses.

He was convinced that sort of approach to the use of grass was a sound one. He was not fearful it would be spoiled because everyone would try and get on the band-waggon in the way that had occurred with barley beef, which had suffered from being too easy to manage.

The Leaths's system called for both stock and pasture management of a high order, 'and the Peter Maclarens of this world are not commonplace figures - a fact which is to the detriment, among other things, of a full exploitation of grassland in Britain.'

USEFUL CONTRIBUTION

Grass alone could not do the job, but, in a combination with barley, it gave the best economic compromise between production per acre, the realisation of calf potential, length of investment and, above all, quality of beef.

The sort of dairy-bred cattle that had been used at The Leaths was not suited to barley beef production because it was too early maturing and lost its capacity to convert concentrated food economically at light weights unless it was subjected to the sort of growth store period that was provided by six months at grass.

The Leaths's work had established clearly that the Ayrshire could make a useful contribution to beef supplies, and that alone was a very important finding. He was not satisfied, however, that the modern beef Shorthorn was the best cross with the Ayrshire, because it did not give the necessary size.

Equally, he was not very happy about the Charolais being used on Ayrshire cows that were being steamed up before calving, that gave them big soft calves that were difficult to rear.

Furthermore, a difficult calving could affect a subsequent lactation, and any gain in the value of the calf might be more than offset by a loss of milk. He wondered whether the North Devon, the Sussex or the Hereford were not a better cross than the Shorthorn. He had experiences of all three crosses with the Ayrshire and, comparably reared, they had more size than the animals they had seen that day. That was a point on which they needed a lot more information, and he hoped it would be the sort of information the Beef Recording Association would provide.

Following Professor Cooper's illuminating address, an interesting discussion ensued on varied aspects of beef production. This was led off by Mr Stephen Williams, a director of Boots Farms Ltd, with replies by the Professor and Mr Maclaren.

APPENDIX 5.
BEEF FROM AYRSHIRES

Speaking practically
by Frank Gerrard

(Newspaper article)

The rapid expansion of the 'Barley Beef' industry has inevitably had the effect of pushing up the price of calves suitable for this type of beef production.

Whereas a few years ago Friesian calves could be bought for about £5 per head, the current figure is approaching £20. The resultant reduction in profit margin has stimulated an interest in the use of other types of calves and other methods of management.

The ICI at their farm in Castle Douglas established a beef production project based upon beef Shorthorn cross calves, out of Ayrshire dairy cows, as far back as 1957. It would appear that a great deal of the success of this venture depends on a good stout beef type Shorthorn bull, capable of balancing up the poor fleshing of the buttocks and loins of the typical Ayrshire cow.

In this particular area, traditionally a stronghold of the Ayrshire breed, there is a ready supply of good quality heifers from known sources. (It is estimated that there are about half a million Ayrshire cattle in Scotland and these could make a considerable contribution to our beef supplies.)

A summary of the performance of 212 animals fattened in 1962-1964 is as follows:

	108 steers	104 heifers
Birth weight (lbs)	77	73
Weight as sold	900	832
Age days	533	549
Daily live-weight gain	1.6	1.4

During the first year, management generally was based upon having the young calves in single pens followed by housing in small groups and then keeping them in large batches. They were then put out to grass. In their second year they reached self-feed silage with some barley and sugar beet pulp. The steers and heifers were separated and grouped for size, and sold as fat, off of silage, during the period of high prices, from about mid-March to the end of May.

Using this method of production, the costing is extremely interesting. Over the 212 animals, the average sale price plus calf subsidy, less the value of the calf, came out at £69, whilst feed, veterinary costs and bedding amount to £3 9s, leaving a gross margin of £38 11s. From these figures a suitable deduction of the common costs for the farm as a whole must be made.

At a demonstration last week carcases of steers and heifers were exhibited from representative animals. One side of beef from each was measured and then cut, in as far as possible a uniform manner, to compare the yield of the various cuts. The following figures were obtained:

	Steer	Heifer
Carcase weight (lb)	526	500
	% side	% side
Valuable cuts	65.9	63.9
K knob	3.6	3.9
H ratio	54	55
Eye muscle length (mm)	133	130
Eye muscle depth (mm)	54	33
Fat over eye (mm)	8	9

These 'valuable cuts' consist of top piece ex-leg; rump and loin ex-k, knob and crop (10 ribs).

There was a ready demand for this type of beef in the Dumfries area and in spite of atrocious weather a group of over 300 farmers (many from overseas) sampled roast beef from similar carcases. It was generally agreed that not only was the meat tender, but it possessed the flavour of 'beef' whilst the fat was mellow and palatable.

INDEX